The quoted ideas expressed in this book (but not scripture verses) are not, in all cases, exact quotations, as some have been edited for clarity and brevity. In all cases, the author has attempted to maintain the speaker's original intent. In some cases, quoted material for this book was obtained from secondary sources, primarily print media. While every effort was made to ensure the accuracy of these sources, the accuracy cannot be guaranteed. For additions, deletions, corrections, or clarifications in future editions of this text, please contact Paul Shepherd, Editor in Chief for Elm Hill Books. Email pshepherd@elmhillbooks.com.

Products from Elm Hill Books may be purchased in bulk for educational, business, fundraising, or sales promotional use. For information, please email SpecialMarkets@ThomasNelson.com.

Scripture quotations are taken from The Holy Bible, King James Version or from:

The Holy Bible, New King James Version (NKJV) Copyright © 1982 by Thomas Nelson, Inc. Used by permission.

New Century Version® (NCV) © 1987, 1988, 1991 by Thomas Nelson, Inc. All rights reserved. Used by permission.

Cover Design by Mark Ross
Page Layout by Bart Dawson

ISBN 1-4041-8495-3

Printed in the United States of America

GOD'S
SURVIVAL GUIDE

FOR WOMEN

TABLE OF CONTENTS

INTRODUCTION

I f you're reading this book, you're probably a woman in search of solutions. Perhaps you have become discouraged with the direction of your life—Perhaps you have almost given up hope. If so, it's time to reconsider. After all, if you're a believer who has entrusted your life to the One from Galilee, you need *never* lose hope.

Wherever you are, no matter how difficult your circumstances, God has a plan for you, a plan that offers renewal, comfort, abundance, and peace. That plan is contained in God's Holy Word, and this book is designed to help you find it.

God has given you a survival guide for life here on earth and life eternal. That guide is the Holy Bible. The Bible is a book unlike any other: it contains God's plan for eternal salvation and His instructions for successful living. As a believer, you are called to study God's Word and to meditate upon its meaning for your life. When you do, you will be enlightened and blessed.

When no one else can comfort you, God can. During those desperate hours between bedtime and dawn, as you fretfully consider the disappointments of a broken past or the dangers of an uncertain future, God offers you a sense of a peace unlike any other. But if you're like most women, you may find it difficult to accept God's peace, especially when your heart is breaking.

This book touches upon 40 topics of intense interest to women. In addition to scriptural resources and essays, the text also contains quote-worthy ideas from notable Christian thinkers.

So, if you sincerely desire to find solutions to life's most difficult questions, don't give up. Instead, keep searching for direction—God's direction. And while you're at it, keep searching for perspective and wisdom—starting with God's wisdom. When you do, you'll discover the comfort, the power, and the peace that only He can give.

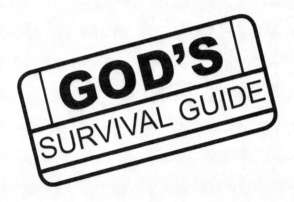

PART I

TAKING CARE OF YOURSELF

Many women naturally assume the role of caregivers while paying scant attention to their own needs. If you're one of those women who spends lots of time caring for others and very little time caring for yourself, please pay careful attention to the ideas that follow.

AGING

We live in a society that glorifies youth. The messages that we receive from the media are unrelenting: We are told that we must do everything within our power to retain youthful values and a youthful appearance. The goal, we are told, is to remain "forever young"—yet this goal is not only unrealistic, it is also unworthy of women who understand what genuine beauty is, and what it isn't.

As you consider what aging means to you, please consider the following:

It's inevitable: Since aging is a fact of life, you should strive to come to terms with it sooner rather than later.

The media focuses on appearances . . . but you should focus on substance, beginning with your spiritual health, your mental health, your physical fitness, and the health of your relationships.

Messages from the media . . . the media is in the business of selling things, so the media wants to convince you that you're not "good enough" until you buy its "new and improved" products. Oftentimes, these products are accompanied by advertisements that make bold promises—promises to stop Father Time in his tracks. These messages are not based upon truth; they're based upon someone's desire to sell you products that you probably don't need . . . so beware.

When it comes to "health and beauty" . . . you should focus more on health than on beauty. In fact, when you take care of your physical, spiritual, and mental health, your appearance will tend to take care of itself.

Talk it over with God: The next time you bow your head in prayer, ask your Heavenly Father if His love is contingent upon your age or appearance. And then, when you've been assured that God loves you during every stage of life, embrace the aging process for what it is: an opportunity to grow closer to your loved ones *and* to your Creator.

Those who are planted in the house of the Lord
Shall flourish in the courts of our God.
They shall still bear fruit in old age;
They shall be fresh and flourishing.

PSALMS 92:13-14 NKJV

To everything there is a season,
a time for every purpose under heaven.

ECCLESIASTES 3:1 NKJV

Older people are wise, and long life brings understanding.

JOB 12:12 NCV

I have carried you since you were born; I have taken care of you from
your birth. Even when you are old, I will be the same. Even when
your hair has turned gray, I will take care of you.
I made you and will take care of you.
I will carry you and save you.

ISAIAH 46:3-4 NCV

And let the beauty of the Lord our God be upon us.

PSALM 90:17 NKJV

It is magnificent to grow old, if one keeps young at heart.

HARRY EMERSON FOSDICK

Don't talk of growing old.
If you continually talk of it, you may bring it on.

HANNAH WHITALL SMITH

As we get older, our vision should improve.
Not our vision of earth, but our vision of heaven.

MAX LUCADO

If you ask me the secret to longevity,
I would tell you that you have to work at taking care of your
health. But, a lot of it is attitude, too.

BESSIE DELANEY

Youth and age touch only the surface of our lives.

C. S. LEWIS

ADDITIONAL BIBLE READINGS

PSALM 37:25; PSALM 71:9; JOB 12:12; ISAIAH 46:3-4

ANXIETY AND PANIC

Ours is an anxious generation. We live in an uncertain world, a world where tragedies can befall the most righteous (and the most innocent) among us. Yet even on those difficult days when our anxieties threaten to overwhelm us, we can be assured that God stands ready to protect us. Psalm 147 promises "He heals the brokenhearted and bandages their wounds" (v. 3, NCV). So, when we are troubled or anxious, we must call upon God, and, in His own time and according to His own plan, He will heal us.

Sometimes, our anxieties may stem from physical causes—chemical reactions in the brain that produce severe emotional distress or crippling panic attacks. In such cases, modern medicine offers hope to those who suffer. But oftentimes, our anxieties result from spiritual deficits, not physical ones. And when we're spiritually depleted, the best prescription is found not in the medicine cabinet but deep inside the human heart. What we need is a higher daily dose of God's love, God's peace, God's assurance, and God's presence. And how do we acquire these blessings from our Creator? Through prayer, through meditation, through worship, and through trust.

Prayer is a powerful antidote to anxiety; so, too, is a regular time of devotional reading and meditation. When we spend quiet moments in the divine presence of our Heavenly Father, we are reminded once again that our troubles are temporary but His love is not.

Worship is yet another tool that can help us overcome the worries and doubts of our anxious age. When we worship God sincerely with our words, with our thoughts, with our prayers, and with our deeds, we are blessed. But the reverse is also true: when we fail to worship God, for whatever reason, we forfeit the spiritual gifts that He intends to be ours.

When Panic Attacks! If you're experiencing intense feelings of anxiety or panic, consult your physician. Medication may be warranted. And remember this: if you're feeling panicky, you are not alone—the National Institute of Mental Health estimates that over 10% of Americans may suffer from some form of anxiety-related disorder during any given year.

God has promised that we may lead lives of abundance, not anxiety. In fact, His Word instructs us to "be anxious for nothing" (Philippians 4:6 NKJV). But how can we put our anxieties to rest? By taking those fears to God and leaving them there.

As you face the challenges of everyday living, do you find yourself becoming anxious, troubled, discouraged, or fearful? If so, turn every one of your concerns over to your Heavenly Father. The same God who created the universe will comfort you if you ask Him...so ask Him and trust Him. And then watch in amazement as your anxieties melt into the warmth of His loving hands.

When you pass through the waters, I will be with you;
and through the rivers, they shall not overflow you.
When you walk through the fire, you shall not be burned,
nor shall the flame scorch you. For I am the Lord your God, The
Holy One of Israel, your Savior.

ISAIAH 43:2-3 NKJV

Therefore do not worry about tomorrow,
for tomorrow will worry about its own things.
Sufficient for the day is its own trouble.

MATTHEW 6:34 NKJV

Be anxious for nothing, but in everything by
prayer and supplication, with thanksgiving,
let your requests be made known to God.

PHILIPPIANS 4:6 NKJV

Anxiety in the heart of man causes depression,
but a good word makes it glad.

PROVERBS 12:25 NKJV

In the multitude of my anxieties within me,
Your comforts delight my soul.

PSALM 94:19 NKJV

God grant me (not my mother-in-law, my child, the neighbor,
or the dog) the serenity (that quiet inner calm) to accept
(not manipulate or tolerate) the things I cannot change
(as much as I would like to), the courage (action in the face of
fear) to change the things I can (people aren't things—
I need to keep telling myself), and the wisdom (knowing
without necessarily knowing how I know) to know
the difference (like when to mind my own business). Amen.

BARBARA JOHNSON

Anxiety is an unnecessary worry. In my opinion,
all worry is unnecessary because it does not help any situation,
and can even make things worse in many cases.

DR. CHARMAINE SAUNDERS

Anxiety does not empty tomorrow of its sorrows,
but it empties today of its strength.

C. H. SPURGEON

ADDITIONAL BIBLE READINGS

PSALM 37:1-2; 1 PETER 5:7-10; PSALM 46:10; PSALM 103:2-4;

LUKE 12:29-31

DEPRESSION

Throughout our lives, all of us must endure personal losses that leave us struggling to find hope. The sadness that accompanies such losses is an inescapable fact of life—but in time, we move beyond our grief as the sadness runs its course and life returns to normal. Depression, however, is more than sadness . . . *much* more.

Depression is a physical and emotional condition that is, in almost all cases, treatable with medication and counseling. And it is not a disease to be taken lightly. Left untreated, depression presents real dangers to patients' physical health and to their emotional wellbeing.

If you're feeling blue, perhaps it's a logical response to the disappointments of everyday life. But if your feelings of sadness have lasted longer than you think they should—or if someone close to you fears that your sadness may have evolved into clinical depression—it's time to seek professional help.

Here are a few simple guidelines to consider as you make decisions about possible medical treatment:

1. If your feelings of sadness have resulted in persistent and prolonged changes in sleep patterns, or if you've experienced a significant change in weight (either gain or loss), consult your physician.

2. If you have persistent urges toward self-destructive behavior, or if you feel as though you have lost the will to live, consult a professional counselor or physician immediately.

3. If someone you trust urges you to seek counseling, schedule a session with a professionally trained counselor to evaluate your condition.

4. If you are plagued by consistent, prolonged, severe feelings of hopelessness, consult a physician, a professional counselor, or your pastor.

God's Word has much to say about every aspect of your life, including your emotional health. And, when you face concerns of any sort—including symptoms of depression—remember that God is with You. Your Creator Father intends that His joy should become your joy. Yet sometimes, amid the inevitable hustle and bustle of life here on earth, you may forfeit—albeit temporarily—God's joy as you wrestle with the challenges of daily living.

So, if you're feeling genuinely depressed, trust your medical doctor to do his or her part. Then, place your ultimate trust in your benevolent Heavenly Father. His healing touch, like His love, endures forever.

But those who wait on the LORD Shall renew their strength;
They shall mount up with wings like eagles,
They shall run and not be weary, They shall walk and not faint.

ISAIAH 40:31 NKJV

Anxiety in the heart of man causes depression,
but a good word makes it glad.

PROVERBS 12:25 NKJV

Yes, we had the sentence of death in ourselves,
that we should not trust in ourselves but in God who raises the dead,
who delivered us from so great a death, and does deliver us;
in whom we trust that He will still deliver us.

2 CORINTHIANS 1:8-10 NKJV

Weeping may endure for a night, but joy comes in the morning.

PSALM 30:5 NKJV

Fear not, for I am with you; Be not dismayed, for I am your God.
I will strengthen you.

ISAIAH 41:10 NKJV

Emotions we have not poured out in the safe hands of God
can turn into feelings of hopelessness and depression.
God is safe.

BETH MOORE

What the devil loves is that vague cloud of unspecified guilt
feeling or unspecified virtue by which he lures us
into despair or presumption.

C. S. LEWIS

The spiritual life is a life beyond moods. It is a life in which
we choose joy and do not allow ourselves to become
victims of passing feelings of happiness or depression.

HENRI NOUWEN

God is good, and heaven is forever.
These two facts should brighten up even the darkest day.

MARIE T. FREEMAN

ADDITIONAL BIBLE READINGS

2 KINGS 20:5; PROVERBS 17:22; PSALM 18:28; PSALM 23; PSALM 43:5

PSALM 56:8; PSALM 143:7-8; PHILIPPIANS 4:8

EATING DISORDERS

O urs is a society that glorifies thinness—to a fault. And as a result, our society is plagued by an epidemic of eating disorders, especially in women. By some estimates, as many as 10% of American women suffer from some form of eating disorder—either self-imposed starvation (a condition known as Anorexia Nervosa), Bulimia (the highly destructive cycle of binge eating and purging), or Binge Eating Disorder (which results in recurrent binge eating not accompanied by purging).

Studies consistently show that the majority of women in America are dissatisfied with their weight and dissatisfied with their appearance. It's no wonder, then, that so many women fall prey to the "3 D's" of weight control: <u>d</u>ieting, <u>d</u>rive for thinness, and body <u>d</u>issatisfaction. As a result, weight loss is *very* big business (Americans are said to spend over 50 billion dollars each year on diet-related products).

> **When food becomes the focus**: If food has become the focus of your life, then food has become your god. Yet the Bible makes it clear that "You shall have no other gods before Me" (Exodus 20:3 NKJV). So ask yourself this question: What will I put first . . . food or God? The answer should be obvious.

Amid this epidemic of weight-related concerns, here are a few things you should know about eating disorders:

Eating disorders are emotionally destructive: The obsession with weight loss can take a terrible emotional toll for women who begin to focus more and more on their appearance.

Eating disorders are always unhealthy and sometimes deadly: All forms of eating disorders do serious damage to the body. Anorexia Nervosa is a particularly deadly condition and should be treated aggressively, immediately, and, if necessary, repeatedly.

Eating disorders are treatable: Treatment is readily available, but many women become so deeply involved in their eating disorders that they simply will not seek treatment. In such cases, family members must step in and seek treatment for the effected person.

If you or someone on your family shows signs of an eating disorder, don't ignore the problem, address the problem. Help is available, and the best day to ask for help is this one.

*You should know that your body is a temple for the Holy Spirit
who is in you. You have received the Holy Spirit from God.
So you do not belong to yourselves, because you were bought by God
for a price. So honor God with your bodies.*

1 CORINTHIANS 6:19-20 NCV

*God does not see the same way people see.
People look at the outside of a person, but the Lord looks at the heart.*

1 SAMUEL 16:7 NCV

*Therefore, whether you eat or drink,
or whatever you do, do all to the glory of God.*

1 CORINTHIANS 10:31 NKJV

*"For I will restore health to you and heal you of your wounds,"
says the Lord.*

JEREMIAH 30:17 NKJV

More Thoughts About . . . DIET AND APPEARANCES

God doesn't use us based on what we look like.
He uses us based on the condition of our souls.

JUDITH COUCHMAN

If the narrative of the Scriptures teaches us anything,
from the serpent in the Garden to the carpenter in Nazareth,
it teaches us that things are rarely what they seem,
that we shouldn't be fooled by appearances.

JOHN ELDREDGE

You will quickly be deceived if you look only to
the outward appearance of men, and you will often
be disappointed if you seek comfort and gain in them.

THOMAS À KEMPIS

The key to healthy eating is common sense and moderation.

JOHN MAXWELL

ADDITIONAL BIBLE READINGS

ROMANS 14:15; ROMANS 14:20; 1 CORINTHIANS 10:31

FORGIVING OTHERS

E ven the most mild-mannered women will, on occasion, have reason to become frustrated by the inevitable shortcomings of family members, friends, and acquaintances. But wise women are quick to forgive others, just as God has forgiven them.

The commandment to forgive is clearly a part of God's Word, but oh how difficult a commandment it can be to follow. Because we are imperfect beings, we are quick to anger, quick to blame, slow to forgive, and even slower to forget. But even when forgiveness is difficult, God's instructions are straightforward: As Christians who have received the gift of forgiveness, we must now share that gift with others.

When we have been injured or embarrassed, we feel

Managing Angry Outbursts

If you think you're about to explode in anger, don't! Instead of striking back at someone, it's usually better to slow down, catch your breath, consider your options, and walk away if you must. Striking out in anger can lead to big problems. So it's better to walk away—and keep walking—than to blurt out angry words that can't be un-blurted.

the urge to strike back and to hurt the people who have hurt us. Christ instructs us to do otherwise. We are taught that forgiveness is God's way and that mercy is an integral part of God's plan for our lives. In short, we are commanded to weave the thread of forgiveness into the very fabric of our lives.

Have you forgiven *all* the people who have done you harm (with no exceptions). If so, you are to be congratulated. But, if you hold bitterness against even a single person—even if that person is no longer living—it's now time to forgive.

Bitterness and regret are not part of God's plan for your life. Forgiveness is. And once you've forgiven others, you can then turn your thoughts to a far more pleasant subject: the incredibly bright future that God has in store for you.

God's Word About . . . **FORGIVING OTHERS**

My dear brothers and sisters, always be willing to listen and slow to speak. Do not become angry easily, because anger will not help you live the right kind of life God wants.

JAMES 1:19–20 NCV

Be kind and loving to each other, and forgive each other just as God forgave you in Christ.

EPHESIANS 4:32 NCV

Smart people are patient; they will be honored if they ignore insults.

PROVERBS 19:11 NCV

If someone does wrong to you, do not pay him back by doing wrong to him. Try to do what everyone thinks is right.

ROMANS 12:17 NCV

Hatred stirs up trouble, but love forgives all wrongs.

PROVERBS 10:12 NCV

Get rid of the poison of built-up anger and the acid
of long-term resentment.

CHARLES SWINDOLL

The fire of anger, if not quenched by loving forgiveness,
will spread and defile and destroy the work of God.

WARREN WIERSBE

Forgiveness is the precondition of love.

CATHERINE MARSHALL

When you harbor bitterness, happiness will dock elsewhere.

ANONYMOUS

ADDITIONAL BIBLE READINGS

ACTS 8:22-23; PSALM 103:3; PSALM 37:7-8; MATTHEW 7:3-5;

MATTHEW 6:14-15; EPHESIANS 4:26-27; PROVERBS 29:22;

HEBREWS 12:14-15; PROVERBS 14:10; JAMES 13:14

FORGIVING YOURSELF

All of us have sinned. Sometimes our sins result from our own stubborn rebellion against God's commandments. Sometimes, we are swept up by events that encourage us to behave in ways that we later come to regret. And sometimes, even when our intentions are honorable, we make mistakes that have long-lasting consequences. When we look back at our actions with remorse, we may experience intense feelings of guilt. But God has an answer for the guilt that we feel. That answer, of course, is His forgiveness.

When we genuinely repent from our wrongdoings, and when we sincerely confess our sins, we are forgiven by our Heavenly Father. But long after God has forgiven us, we may continue to withhold forgiveness from ourselves. Instead of accepting God's mercy and accepting our past, we may think long and hard—far too long and hard—about the things that "might have been," the things that "could have been," or the things that "should have been."

Are you a woman who is troubled by feelings of guilt, even after you've received God's forgiveness? Are you still struggling with painful memories of mistakes you made long ago? Are you focused so intently on yesterday that your vision of today is clouded? If so, you still have work to do—spiritual work. You should ask your Heavenly Father not for forgiveness (He granted that gift the very first time you asked Him!) but instead for acceptance and trust: acceptance of the past and trust in God's plan for your life.

Once you have asked God for His forgiveness, you can be certain that your Heavenly Father has given it. And if He, in His infinite wisdom, will forgive your sins, how then can you withhold forgiveness from yourself? The answer, of course, is that once God has forgiven you, you should forgive yourself, too.

When you forgive yourself thoroughly and completely, you'll stop investing energy in those most useless of emotions: bitterness, regret, and self-recrimination. And you can then get busy making the world a better place, and that's as it should be. After all, since God has forgiven you, it's it about time for you to demonstrate your gratitude by serving Him?

---

*If we confess our sins, He is faithful and just to forgive us our sins
and to cleanse us from all unrighteousness.*

1 JOHN 1:9 NKJV

*Let us, then, feel very sure that we can come before God's throne
where there is grace. There we can receive mercy and grace
to help us when we need it.*

HEBREWS 4:16 NCV

*There is therefore now no condemnation to those who are in
Christ Jesus, who do not walk according to the flesh,
but according to the Spirit.*

ROMANS 8:1 NKJV

*All the prophets say it is true that all who believe in Jesus
will be forgiven of their sins through Jesus' name.*

ACTS 10:43 NCV

*Whoever is wise will observe these things, and they will understand
the lovingkindness of the Lord.*

PSALM 107:43 NKJV

When God forgives, He forgets.
He buries our sins in the sea and puts a sign on the shore saying,
"No Fishing Allowed."

CORRIE TEN BOOM

There is nothing, absolutely nothing, that God will not forgive.
You cannot "out-sin" His forgiveness.
You cannot "out-sin" the love of God.

KATHY TROCCOLI

I think that if God forgives us we might forgive ourselves.
Otherwise it is almost like setting up ourselves
as a higher tribunal than Him.

C. S. LEWIS

If you can't forgive yourself,
you're saying Christ didn't do enough.

ANONYMOUS

ADDITIONAL BIBLE READINGS

MATTHEW 9:12-13; PSALM 51:5-7; PSALM 32:5

GRIEF

Grief visits all of us who live long and love deeply. When we lose a loved one, or when we experience any other profound loss, darkness overwhelms us for a while, and it seems as if our purpose for living has vanished. Thankfully, God has other plans.

The Christian faith, as communicated through the words of the Holy Bible, is a healing faith. It offers comfort in times of trouble, courage for our fears, hope instead of hopelessness. For Christians, the grave is not a final resting-place, it is a place of transition. Through the healing words of God's promises, Christians understand that the Lord continues to manifest His plan in good times and bad.

God intends that you have a meaningful, abundant life, but He expects you to do your part in claiming those blessings. So, as you work through your grief, you will find it helpful to utilize all the resources that God has placed along your path. God makes help available, but it's up to you to find it and then to accept it.

First and foremost, you should lean upon the love, help, and support of family members, friends, fellow church members, and your pastor. Other resources include:

• Various local counseling services including, but not limited to, pastoral counselors, psychologists, and community mental health facilities.

- Group counseling programs which may deal with your specific loss.
- Your personal physician.
- The local bookstore or library (which will contain specific reading material about your grief and about your particular loss).

If you are experiencing the intense pain of a recent loss, or if you are still mourning a loss from long ago, Perhaps you are now ready to begin the next stage of your journey with God. If so, be mindful of this fact: As a wounded survivor, you will have countless opportunities to serve others. And by serving others, you will bring purpose and meaning to the suffering you've endured.

The Grief of Miscarriage

If you've suffered a miscarriage, you're already aware that the emotional impact of your loss can be devastating. So it's not surprising that your complete emotional recovery may take years. Indeed some losses, especially the loss of a child, can change a woman forever. But remember this: no grief is too big for God—not even yours.

As you look back upon your miscarriage, you may experience intense anger: anger at your caregivers, anger at yourself, or even anger at your God. Although feelings of anger may be an inevitable part of the grieving process, you must not allow those hurtful feelings to become a *permanent* part of your emotional makeup. God has better things in store for you! And if you petition Him prayerfully and often, He will—in His own time and in His own way—help you move beyond your feelings of grief to a place of acceptance and peace.

God's Word About . . . **GRIEF**

---

*Therefore let those who suffer according to the will of God
commit their souls to Him in doing good,
as to a faithful Creator.*

1 PETER 4:19 NKJV

You will be sad, but your sadness will become joy.

JOHN 16:20 NCV

Blessed are those who mourn, for they shall be comforted.

MATTHEW 5:4 NKJV

This is my comfort in my affliction, for Your word has given me life.

PSALM 119:50 NKJV

*"Death, where is your victory? Death, where is your pain?"
Death's power to hurt is sin, and the power of sin is the law.
But we thank God! He gives us the victory through
our Lord Jesus Christ.*

1 CORINTHIANS 15:55–57 NCV

More Thoughts About . . . **GRIEF**

Mercy is not the ability to no longer feel the pain and heartache of living in this world. Mercy is knowing that I am being held through the pain by my Father.

ANGELA THOMAS

Suffering may be someone's fault or it may not be anyone's fault. But if given to God, our suffering becomes an opportunity to experience the power of God at work in our lives and to give glory to Him.

ANNE GRAHAM LOTZ

I am not a theologian or a scholar, but I am very aware of the fact that pain is necessary to all of us. In my own life, I think I can honestly say that out of the deepest pain has come the strongest conviction of the presence of God and the love of God.

ELISABETH ELLIOT

Even in the winter, even in the midst of the storm, the sun is still there. Somewhere, up above the clouds, it still shines and warms and pulls at the life buried deep inside the brown branches and frozen earth. The sun is there! Spring will come.

GLORIA GAITHER

ADDITIONAL BIBLE READINGS

ROMANS 5:3-4; REVELATION 21:4; PSALM 23; PSALM 56:13;

PSALM116:1-4

INFERTILITY

Infertility is generally defined as a couple's inability to achieve a pregnancy after trying for 12 months. The causes of infertility are numerous, and, thankfully, so are the treatments.

Estimates indicate that 10% to 20% of couples are unable to conceive a child during their first year. If that statistic describes you, then your choices include:

Medical intervention: infertility has many causes, and modern medicine has developed almost as many solutions. If you and your husband are considering medical options, your primary care physicians can refer you in the right direction.

Adoption: Perhaps God's plan for you and your husband includes the adoption of a child. If you feel led in this direction, pray about it—and keep praying as you explore the many options that are available to couples who want to adopt.

Waiting Patiently: Perhaps the thing that you and your husband need most is simply a little more patience. God's Word advises, "Rest in the Lord, and wait patiently for Him" (Psalm 37:7 NKJV). Sometimes, God's timing is far different from your own, but if you sincerely seek to be a woman of faith, then you must learn to trust God . . . and you must learn to wait patiently for Him.

Wait on the LORD; Be of good courage,
and He shall strengthen your heart; Wait, I say, on the LORD!

PSALM 27:14 NKJV

But those who wait on the LORD Shall renew their strength;
They shall mount up with wings like eagles,
They shall run and not be weary, They shall walk and not faint.

ISAIAH 40:31 NKJV

He has made everything beautiful in its time.
Also He has put eternity in their hearts, except that no one
can find out the work that God does from beginning to end.

ECCLESIASTES 3:11 NKJV

I say this because I know what I am planning for you,"
says the Lord. "I have good plans for you, not plans to hurt you.
I will give you hope and a good future."

JEREMIAH 29:11 NCV

Therefore humble yourselves under the mighty hand of God,
that He may exalt you in due time.

1 PETER 5:6 NKJV

God is working in you to help you want to do and be able to do
what pleases him.

PHILIPPIANS 2:13 NCV

People may make plans in their minds,
but the Lord decides what they will do.

PROVERBS 16:9 NCV

For with God nothing will be impossible.

LUKE 1:37 NKJV

Waiting on God brings us to the journey's end quicker
than our feet.

MRS. CHARLES E. COWMAN

He whose attitude towards Christ is correct does indeed ask
"in His Name" and receives what he asks for if it is something
which does not stand in the way of his salvation. He gets it,
however, only when he ought to receive it, for certain things are
not refused us, but their granting is delayed to a fitting time.

ST. AUGUSTINE

It's safe to trust God's methods and to go by His clock.

S. D. GORDON

Will not the Lord's time be better than your time?

C. H. SPURGEON

ADDITIONAL BIBLE READINGS

1 SAMUEL 1:11; ISAIAH 55:8-9; ROMANS 8:28; LUKE 1:13

MENOPAUSE

Menopause—the period in a woman's life when her body produces less estrogen and progesterone—marks the decrease and eventual cessation of menstruation. Menopause is naturally-occurring event that typically takes place between the ages of 45 and 55.

Although every woman experiences menopause differently, many symptoms are commonplace. Those symptoms may include:

Mood Swings: you may experience emotions that are unfamiliar to you. These emotions may range from slight irritability to intense feelings of anger or depression.

Sleep disturbances: you may awaken from sleep with soaking night sweats and chills. Or, you may find that restful sleep is difficult to achieve. And your lack of sleep may have an impact on your moods.

> **The world continues to change, as do we.** Change is inevitable—we can either roll *with* it or be rolled over *by* it. In order to avoid the latter, we should choose the former . . . and trust God as we go.

Physical Changes: As your estrogen level drops, you may notice changes in your physical appearance. These changes may be somewhat troubling to you, but you should remember that these physical changes are simply part of the natural aging process.

Before, during, and after menopause, you should see your physician regularly. Together, you and your doctor can consider the various therapies are available to lessen the physical and emotional impact of menopause.

This is why I remind you to keep using the gift
God gave you when I laid my hands on you.
Now let it grow, as a small flame grows into a fire.

2 TIMOTHY 1:6 NCV

*To everything there is a season,
a time for every purpose under heaven.*

ECCLESIASTES 3:1 NKJV

So teach us to number our days, that we may gain a heart of wisdom.

PSALM 90:12 NKJV

Older people are wise, and long life brings understanding.

JOB 12:12 NCV

*Or do you not know that your body is the temple
of the Holy Spirit who is in you?*

1 CORINTHIANS 6:19 NKJV

This is the day the LORD has made; we will rejoice and be glad in it.

PSALM 118:24 NKJV

___

Conditions are always changing; therefore,
I must not be dependent upon conditions.
What matters supremely is my soul and
my relationship to God.

CORRIE TEN BOOM

With God, it isn't who you were that matters;
it's who you are becoming.

LIZ CURTIS HIGGS

Ask the God who made you to keep remaking you.

NORMAN VINCENT PEALE

In a world kept chaotic by change, you will eventually discover,
as I have, that this is one of the most precious qualities
of the God we are looking for: He doesn't change.

BILL HYBELS

___

ADDITIONAL BIBLE READINGS

PSALM 92:13-14; ECCLESIASTES 3:1-8; ISAIAH 40:31

MENTAL HEALTH

Thoughts are intensely powerful things. Your thoughts have the power to lift you up or drag you down; they have the power to energize you or deplete you, the power to inspire you to accomplish great things, or the power to make those accomplishments impossible. That's why you must carefully guard your mental and emotional health.

God intends that you experience joy and abundance, but He will not force His joy upon you; you must claim it for yourself. It's up to you to celebrate the life that God has given you by focusing your mind upon "whatever is commendable" (Philippians 4:7-8). But if your psyche is plagued by intense feelings of depression or anxiety, you will not be able to focus on the "commendable" aspects of life.

For previous generations, mental illness was largely a mystery. But today, thanks to remarkable advances in medicine, we know that each human brain (including yours) is a highly complex system that should be treated with the utmost care—which means proper diet, sufficient rest, and the strict avoidance of harmful substances.

God intends for you to treat you body like a temple (1 Corinthians 3:16). And because your brain is an integral part of your body, your brain, too, deserves to be cared for as if it were a sacred place . . . which, by the way, it is.

Concerned about metal health? Treatment in available: some folks are still reluctant to discuss—much less confront—issues of mental health. You, however, should *never* be afraid to communicate your concerns about your own mental health *or* the mental health of someone you love. Whom should you talk to? You can begin by talking things over with your physician and your pastor. Treatment is readily available for maladies such as depression or anxiety. So at the first sign of trouble, don't ignore the problem; start taking steps to solve it.

But Jesus turned around, and when He saw her He said,
"Be of good cheer, daughter; your faith has made you well."
And the woman was made well from that hour.

MATTHEW 9:22 NKJV

Listen carefully to wisdom; set your mind on understanding.

PROVERBS 2:2 NCV

Jesus answered, "Love the Lord your God with all your heart,
all your soul, and all your mind."
This is the first and most important command.

MATTHEW 22:37-38 NCV

And the peace of God, which surpasses all understanding,
will guard your hearts and minds through Christ Jesus.
Finally, brethren, whatever things are true, whatever things are noble,
whatever things are just, whatever things are pure,
whatever things are lovely, whatever things are of good report,
if there is any virtue and if there is anything praiseworthy—
meditate on these things.

PHILIPPIANS 4:7-8 NKJV

Finally, all of you be of one mind, having compassion for
one another; love as brothers, be tenderhearted, be courteous.

1 PETER 3:8 NKJV

The world's sewage system threatens to contaminate
the stream of Christian thought.
Is the world shaping your mind, or is Christ?

BILLY GRAHAM

No more imperfect thoughts. No more sad memories.
No more ignorance. My redeemed body will have
a redeemed mind. Grant me a foretaste of that perfect mind
as you mirror your thoughts in me today.

JONI EARECKSON TADA

The things we think are the things that feed our souls.
If we think on pure and lovely things, we shall grow pure and
lovely like them; and the converse is equally true.

HANNAH WHITALL SMITH

Your thoughts are the determining factor as to whose mold you
are conformed to. Control your thoughts and
you control the direction of your life.

CHARLES STANLEY

ADDITIONAL BIBLE READINGS

ROMANS 12:1-2; MATTHEW 5:8; JAMES 4:8; 2 TIMOTHY 1:7;

PSALM 9:9; PSALM 107:20; PROVERBS 3:24-26

PRIORITIES AND BALANCE

Has the busy pace of life robbed you of the peace of mind that should rightfully be yours? Has a bloated to-do list left you with little time for yourself and even less time for your loved ones? Are you so busy running from place to place that you scarcely have time to ask yourself where you're running—or why? If so, then you—like so many women who are trying to make ends meet here in the 21st Century—are simply too busy for your own good.

Time is a nonrenewable gift from God. How will you use it? You know from experience that you should invest some time each day in yourself, but finding time to do so is easier said than done. Why? Because so many people are expecting so many things from you!

You live in a noisy world, a world filled with distractions, frustrations, temptations, and obligations. But if you allow the distractions of everyday life to distract you from God's peace, you're doing yourself a big disservice. So here's some good advice: instead of rushing nonstop through the day, slow yourself down long enough to have a few quiet minutes with God.

An important element of your stewardship to God is the way that you choose to spend the time He has entrusted to you. Each waking moment holds the potential to help a friend, to hug a child, to say a kind word, or to think a noble thought. Your challenge, as a believer, is to value your time, to use it judiciously, and to use it in ways that honor your Heavenly Father.

If you're having trouble prioritizing your day, perhaps you've been trying to organize your life according to your own plans, not God's. A better strategy, of course, is to take your daily obligations and place them in the hands of the One who created you. To do so, you must prioritize your day according to God's commandments, and you must seek His will and His wisdom in all matters. Then, you can face the day with the assurance that the same God who created our universe out of nothingness will help you place first things first in your own life.

As you establish priorities for your day and your life, remember that each new day is a special treasure to be savored and celebrated. As a Christian, you have much to celebrate and much to do. Every day, like every life, is composed of moments. Each moment offers you the potential to seek God's will and to serve His purposes. If you are wise, you will strive to do both.

Each day is a special treasure to be savored and celebrated. May you—as a Christian woman who has so much to celebrate— never fail to praise your Creator by rejoicing in this glorious day, and by using it wisely.

---

*Come to Me, all you who labor and are heavy laden,
and I will give you rest. Take My yoke upon you and learn from Me,
for I am gentle and lowly in heart, and you will find rest for
your souls. For My yoke is easy and My burden is light.*

MATTHEW 11:28-30 NKJV

*Then the apostles gathered to Jesus and told Him all things, both
what they had done and what they had taught. And He said to them,
"Come aside by yourselves to a deserted place and rest a while."
For there were many coming and going, and they did not
even have time to eat.*

MARK 6: 30-31 NKJV

*Now it happened as they went that He entered a certain village;
and a certain woman named Martha welcomed Him into her house.
And she had a sister called Mary, who also sat at Jesus' feet and
heard His word. But Martha was distracted with much serving,
and she approached Him and said, "Lord, do You not care that
my sister has left me to serve alone? Therefore tell her to help me."
And Jesus answered and said to her, "Martha, Martha,
you are worried and troubled about many things.
But one thing is needed, and Mary has chosen that good part,
which will not be taken away from her."*

LUKE 10:38-42 NKJV

Every one of us is supposed to be a powerhouse for God,
living in balance and harmony within and without.

JOYCE MEYER

Frustration is not the will of God.
There is time to do anything and everything
that God wants us to do.

ELISABETH ELLIOT

Great relief and satisfaction can come from seeking
God's priorities for us in each season, discerning what is "best"
in the midst of many noble opportunities,
and pouring our most excellent energies into those things.

BETH MOORE

Have you prayed about your resources lately?
Find out how God wants you to use your time and your money.
No matter what it costs, forsake all that is not of God.

KAY ARTHUR

Give God what's right—not what's left!

ANONYMOUS

ADDITIONAL BIBLE READINGS

ISAIAH 40:31; MATTHEW 6:33; MATTHEW 11:28-30;

LUKE 10:38-42

SELF-IMAGE

Do you like the person you see when you look into the mirror? You should! After all, the person in the mirror is a very special person who is made—and loved—by God. And God knew precisely what He was doing when He gave you a unique set of talents and opportunities. Now, it's up to you to discover those talents and to use them, but sometimes the world will encourage you to do otherwise. At times, society will attempt to force you into a particular, preformed mold. Yet God may have other plans in store for you.

The world will attempt to define you—how you should look, how you should act, and how you should think. And, because you're an imperfect human being, you may become so wrapped up in meeting the world's expectations that you fail to focus on God's expectations. To do so is a mistake of major proportions—don't make it. Instead of trying to please the world, try to please God (by becoming the very best "you" that you can possibly be).

Thousands of books have been written about ways to improve self-esteem. Yet, maintaining a healthy self-image is, to a surprising extent, a matter of doing three things: 1. Obeying God 2. Thinking healthy thoughts 3. Finding a purpose for your life that pleases your Creator and yourself. The following ideas can help you build the kind of self-image—and the kind of life—that both you and God can be proud of:

Behave yourself: If you're not behaving yourself, how can you possibly expect to feel good about yourself? (1 Peter 3:12)

Guard your thoughts and guard your heart: Even though you can't control every thought, you can usually control the direction of your thoughts. (Philippians 4:8)

Spend time with people who are upbeat, enthusiastic, and encouraging. If you and your friends always seem to end up in "the critic's corner," it's time to find new friends . . . and a new corner! (James 4:11)

Don't be too hard on yourself: If you're willing to forgive other people's mistakes, then you should be willing to forgive your own mistakes, too. (Romans 14:22)

Find something that you're passionate about: Become so wrapped up in something that you simply don't have the time to worry about self-esteem. (Colossians 3:23)

Beware of addictions: Addictions, of whatever type, lead to misery, grief, and low self-esteem. (Exodus 20:3)

Finally, here's a word of caution: don't spend too much time focusing on self-esteem: Instead, you should focus on using your talents and pleasing your God. You should learn to direct your thoughts in positive ways. You should strive to find something to do and someone to love. When you accomplish these things, your self-esteem will, on most days, take care of itself.

For we are His workmanship, created in Christ Jesus for good works, which God prepared beforehand that we should walk in them.

EPHESIANS 2:10 NKJV

For You formed my inward parts; You covered me in my mother's womb. I will praise You, for I am fearfully and wonderfully made; Marvelous are Your works.

PSALM 139:13-14 NKJV

For You have made him a little lower than the angels, And You have crowned him with glory and honor.

PSALM 8:5 NKJV

God began doing a good work in you, and I am sure he will continue it until it is finished when Jesus Christ comes again.

PHILIPPIANS 1:6 NCV

Whether we find ourselves overworking, overspending,
overparenting—whatever we choose as our obsession—
there is a valuable freedom found when we can accept that
our worth is not based on what we do, how we do it,
or what others think of us.

ANNIE CHAPMAN

Everyone has inside himself a piece of good news!
The good news is that you really don't know how great
you can be, now much you can live, what you can accomplish,
and what your potential is.

ANNE FRANK

I may have tasted peace, but to believe that the God of heaven
and earth calls me beautiful—well, I think I could rest in that.
If I truly knew that He was smitten with me,
maybe I could take a deep breath, square my shoulders,
and go out to face the world with confidence.

ANGELA THOMAS

Find satisfaction in him who made you, and only then
find satisfaction in yourself as part of his creation.

ST. AUGUSTINE

ADDITIONAL BIBLE READINGS

ECCLESIASTES 11:4, 6; 2 TIMOTHY 1:6

WEIGHT-RELATED ISSUES

We live in a society that is obsessed with thinness. Yet ours is a fast-food world where fattening foods are convenient, inexpensive, tempting, and popular. To make matters worse, ours is a digital society filled with modern conveniences that can rob us of the physical exercise we need to maintain healthy lifestyles.

As adults, each of us bears a personal responsibility for the general state of our own physical health. Certainly, various aspects of health are beyond our control: illness sometimes strikes even the healthiest men and women. But for most of us, physical health is a choice: it is the result of hundreds of small decisions that we make every day of our lives. If we make decisions that promote good health, our bodies respond. But if we fall into bad habits and undisciplined lifestyles, we suffer tragic consequences.

It's your body. Do you sincerely desire to improve your physical health? If so, start by taking personal responsibility for the body that God has given you. Then, make the solemn pledge to yourself that you will begin to make the changes that are required to enjoy a longer, healthier, happier life. No one can make those changes for you; you must make them for yourself. And with God's help, you can . . . and you will.

When our unhealthy habits lead to poor health, we find it all too easy to look beyond ourselves and assign blame. But to blame others is to miss the point: we, and we alone, are responsible for the way that we treat our bodies. And the sooner that we accept that responsibility, the sooner we can assert control over our bodies and our lives.

> **Striving to be rail-thin?** Don't equate thinness with happiness. You need not be rail-thin to be happy, healthy, and well adjusted. And don't be obsessive about your diet; your life shouldn't revolve around food.

Over the years our bodies become walking autobiographies, telling friends and strangers alike of the minor and major stresses of our lives.

MARILYN FERGUSON

God's Word About ... **SELF-DISCIPLINE AND HEALTH**

> *Learn the truth and never reject it.*
> *Get wisdom, self-control, and understanding.*

PROVERBS 23:23 NCV

> *But I discipline my body and bring it into subjection, lest,*
> *when I have preached to others, I myself should become disqualified.*

1 CORINTHIANS 9:27 NKJV

> *I beseech you therefore, brethren, by the mercies of God, that you*
> *present your bodies a living sacrifice, holy, acceptable to God, which*
> *is your reasonable service. And do not be conformed to this world,*
> *but be transformed by the renewing of your mind, that you may*
> *prove what is that good and acceptable and perfect will of God.*

ROMANS 12:1-2 NKJV

> *Beloved, I pray that you may prosper in all things and be in health,*
> *just as your soul prospers.*

3 JOHN 1:2 NKJV

> *A happy heart is like good medicine.*

PROVERBS 17:22 NCV

More Thoughts About . . . **SELF-DISCIPLINE**

The habit of self-control is not easily acquired,
but totally necessary.

FANNY JACKSON COPPIN

It doesn't matter what you're trying to accomplish.
It's all a matter of discipline.

WILMA RUDOLPH

Your thoughts are the determining factor as to whose mold you
are conformed to. Control your thoughts and
you control the direction of your life.

CHARLES STANLEY

As we seek to become disciples of Jesus Christ, we should
never forget that the word disciple is directly related to
the word discipline. To be a disciple of the Lord
Jesus Christ is to be disciplined.

DENNIS SWANBERG

ADDITIONAL BIBLE READINGS

MATTHEW 9:22; PSALM 27:1; PSALM 42:11; EPHESIANS 4:23-24;

I CORINTHIANS 6:19-20; PROVERBS 3:7-8

WORRY

I f you are like most women, it's simply a fact of life: from time to time, you worry. You worry about health, about finances, about safety, about relationships, about family, and about countless other challenges of life, some great and some small.

Because of His humanity, Jesus understood the inevitability of worry. And he addressed the topic clearly and forcefully in the 6th chapter of Matthew:

> *Therefore I say to you, do not worry about your life, what you will eat or what you will drink; nor about your body, what you will put on. Is not life more than food and the body more than clothing? Look at the birds of the air, for they neither sow nor reap nor gather into barns; yet your heavenly Father feeds them. Are you not of more value than they? Which of you by worrying can add one cubit to his stature? . . . Therefore do not worry about tomorrow, for tomorrow will worry about its own things. Sufficient for the day is its own trouble.* (v. 25-27, 34 NKJV)

More often than not, our worries stem from an inability to focus and to trust. We fail to focus on a priceless gift from God: the profound, precious, present moment. Instead of thanking God for the blessings of this day, we choose to fret about two more ominous days: yesterday and tomorrow. We stew about the unfairness of the past, or we agonize about the uncertainty of the future. Such thinking stirs up negative feelings that prepare our hearts and minds for an equally destructive emotion: fear.

Our fears are also rooted in a failure to trust. Instead of trusting God's plans for our lives, we fix our minds on countless troubles that might come to pass (but seldom do). A better strategy, of course, is to take God at His word by trusting His promises. Our Lord has promised that He will care for our needs—needs, by the way, that He understands far more completely than we do. God's Word is unambiguous; so, too, should be our trust in Him.

In Matthew 6, Jesus reminds us that each day has enough worries of its own without the added weight of yesterday's regrets or tomorrow's fears. That's a message worth remembering. So the next time you're tempted to worry about the mistakes of yesterday or the uncertainties of tomorrow, turn your heart toward God. Take your troubles to Him; take your fears to Him; take your doubts to Him; take your weaknesses to Him; take your sorrows to Him . . . and leave them all there. Seek protection from the One who offers you eternal salvation; build your spiritual house upon the Rock that cannot be moved.

I was very worried, but you comforted me . . . .

PSALM 94:19 NCV

Give your worries to the Lord, and he will take care of you.
He will never let good people down.

PSALM 55:22 NCV

Do not worry about anything,
but pray and ask God for everything you need,
always giving thanks.

PHILIPPIANS 4:6 NCV

Therefore do not worry about tomorrow,
for tomorrow will worry about its own things.
Sufficient for the day is its own trouble.

MATTHEW 6:34 NKJV

Worry does not empty tomorrow of its sorrow;
it empties today of its strength.

CORRIE TEN BOOM

Today is mine. Tomorrow is none of my business.
If I peer anxiously into the fog of the future,
I will strain my spiritual eyes so that I will not see
clearly what is required of me now.

ELISABETH ELLIOTT

Worry is a cycle of inefficient thoughts whirling around
a center of fear.

CORRIE TEN BOOM

Remember always that there are two things
which are more utterly incompatible even than oil and water,
and these two are trust and worry.

HANNAH WHITALL SMITH

ADDITIONAL BIBLE READINGS

JOHN 14:27; JOHN 14:1; PSALM 55: 22; PSALM 56:11; PSALM 84:11;

PSALM 118:8-9

PART II

CARING FOR YOUR LOVED ONES

The beautiful words of 1st Corinthians 13 remind us that we are commanded by God to love others: "And now abide faith, hope, love, these three; but the greatest of these is love" (v.13, NKJV). Faith is important, of course. So, too, is hope. But, love is more important still. Christ showed His love for us on the cross, and, as Christians, we are called upon to return Christ's love by sharing it. In Part II of this text, we consider how best to help those we love.

AGING PARENTS

Caring for aging parents demands heaping helpings of patience, discretion, diplomacy, perseverance, gentleness, strength, compassion, wisdom, and, most importantly, love. If you're responsible, either directly or indirectly, for the care of an elderly parent, you already know that it's challenging job. But you also know that caring for your loved ones is not only a responsibility; it's also a privilege.

Because every family is different, easy solutions can be elusive, but the following strategies can help:

Make the Golden Rule Your Rule: Do unto your parents as you will want you children to do unto you. (Matthew 7:12)

Don't be in such a hurry: even if you're a very busy woman, you should never be too busy to spend a few moments with your parents.

Avoid angry outbursts: Sweet words usually work better than sour ones. (Proverbs 19:11)

Pray about it and keep praying about it: God has answers, and God answers prayer . . . so keep praying! (James 5:16)

Take an Active Role: As the old saying goes, there are three kinds of people: people who *make* things happen, people who *wait* for things to happen, and people who scratch their heads and ask, *"What happened?"* When it comes to caring for your aging parent, you should be the kind of person who makes things happen.

Take Care of Yourself: Caring for an aging parent can be physically demanding and emotionally draining. So, get plenty of rest, and don't forget to eat your Wheaties₀. (Matthew 11:28-30)

Honor God by Honoring Them: God wants you to honor your parents, and when you do, you also honor Him. (Exodus 20:12)

At times, the duty of caring for aging parents may seem like a thankless task, but it is not. Even if your parents can't fully appreciate your sacrifices, God does. And of this you may be certain: The Lord will find surprising ways to reward your faithfulness.

Let them first learn to do their duty to their own family and
to repay their parents or grandparents.
That pleases God.

1 TIMOTHY 5:4 NCV

Honor your father and your mother,
that your days may be long upon the land
which the Lord your God is giving you.

EXODUS 20:12 NKJV

Every kingdom divided against itself is brought to desolation,
and every city or house divided against itself will not stand.

MATTHEW 12:25 NKJV

Old people are proud of their grandchildren,
and children are proud of their parents.

PROVERBS 17:6 NCV

We need to turn to Jesus Christ for wisdom
as we relate to our parents.

DENNIS SWANBERG

What can we do to promote world peace?
Go home and love your family.

MOTHER TERESA

The only true source of meaning in life is found in love for
God and his son Jesus Christ, and love for mankind,
beginning with our own families.

JAMES DOBSON

Every Christian family ought to be, as it were, a little church,
consecrated to Christ, and wholly influenced and
governed by His rules.

JONATHAN EDWARDS

ADDITIONAL BIBLE READINGS

DEUTERONOMY 5:16; PROVERBS 28:24; PROVERBS 23-25; I PETER 5:5

CARING FOR YOUNG CHILDREN

I f you're caring for a young child, you already know that the demands of being a mother can seem overwhelming at times. Yet even on those days when the house is in an uproar, the laundry is piled high, and the bills are piled even higher, wise mothers never forget their overriding goal: shaping the minds and hearts of their children.

Thoughtful mothers (like you) understand the critical importance of raising their children with love, with family, with discipline, and with God. By making God a focus in the home, loving mothers offer a priceless legacy to their children—a legacy of hope, a legacy of love, and a legacy of wisdom.

Your child is a gift from the Creator, a priceless treasure that the Father has entrusted to your care. As you consider the best ways to care for your child, the following Biblically-based principles can be helpful:

1. **Love is the foundation**: When it comes to raising our kids, the words from 1 Corinthians 13:13 certainly apply: "And now abide faith, hope, love, these three; but the greatest of these is love." Every child deserves to grow up in a safe, loving, God-fearing home, and it's up to you to make certain that your home fits that description.

2. **Words are never enough**: When it comes to teaching our children, the things we say pale in comparison to the things we do.

3. **Safety, safety, safety**: As a responsible parent, it's up to you to be your family's safety expert. Impulsive kids, left to their own devices, tend to get themselves into dangerous situations; responsible adults, however, don't leave kids to their own devices.

4. **Allow your child to experience logical consequences**: The world won't protect your child from the consequences of misbehavior, and neither should you. As a parent, your job is to ensure that the consequences of your child's actions are logical, measured, appropriate, and thoroughly understood by your youngster.

5. **Listen first, then speak**: For most parents, the temptation to lecture is great; it takes conscious effort to hold one's tongue until one's ears are fully engaged. When a parent is able to do so, his or her efforts are usually rewarded.

6. **Ask lots of questions**: When questions can be answered with a simple "yes" or "no," youngsters will tend to answer accordingly; a better strategy is to ask questions that require a more thoughtful response. Such questions might begin

with: "How do you feel about…" or "What do you think about…".

7. **Be Creative**: There are many ways to say, "I love you." Find them. Put love notes in lunch pails and on pillows; hug relentlessly; laugh and play with abandon.

8. **Share your faith**: You need not have attended seminary to have worthwhile opinions about your faith. Express those opinions, especially to your children. Your kids need to know where you stand.

9. **No matter how busy you are, make time for your children.** Chuck Swindoll has this simple advice: "Never give your family the leftovers and crumbs of your time." And he's right.

10. **Put God first in every aspect of your life.** And while you're at it, put Him first in every aspect of your family's life, too. (Joshua 24:15)

As Jesus was walking along, he saw a man
who had been born blind. His followers asked him,
"Teacher, whose sin caused this man to be born
blind—his own sin or his parents' sin?"
Jesus answered, "It is not this man's sin or
his parents' sin that made him be blind.
This man was born blind so that
God's power could be shown in him."

JOHN 9:1-3 NCV

*The good people who live honest lives will be
a blessing to their children.*

PROVERBS 20:7 NCV

*Therefore you shall lay up these words of mine in your heart and
in your soul . . . . You shall teach them to your children,
speaking of them when you sit in your house, when you walk by
the way, when you lie down, and when you rise up.*

DEUTERONOMY 11:18-19 NKJV

*My son, hear the instruction of your father,
And do not forsake the law of your mother.*

PROVERBS 1:8 NKJV

*Train up a child in the way he should go,
and when he is old he will not depart from it.*

PROVERBS 22:6 NKJV

Every child born into the world is a new thought of God,
an ever-fresh and radiant possibility.

KATE DOUGLAS WIGGIN

Children are not casual guests in our home.
They have been loaned to us temporarily for the purpose of
loving them and instilling a foundation of values on
which their future lives will be built.

JAMES DOBSON

Children are the hands by which we take hold of heaven.

HENRY WARD BEECHER

Our faithfulness, or lack of it, will have an overwhelming impact
on the heritage of our children.

BETH MOORE

ADDITIONAL BIBLE READINGS

MARK 9:36-37; MATTHEW 18:2-3; 1 CORINTHIANS 13:1-13;

EXODUS 4:11

DATING

If you're a single woman, you know from firsthand experience that "the dating game" can be quite a painful game to play! Perhaps you've never been married. Or perhaps you've been reintroduced to the dating world after years of married life. In either case, you'll probably agree that finding the right man can be, at times, an exercise in trial and error—with a heavy emphasis on error.

If you've already discovered "Mr. Perfect," thank the Good Lord for your good fortune. But if you're still looking, here are some things to consider:

1. **Put God first**: God should come first in every aspect of your life, including your dating life: He deserves first place, and any relationship that doesn't put Him there is the wrong relationship for you. (Exodus 20:3)

2. **Be contented where you are, even if it's not exactly where you want to end up**: Think about it like this: maybe God has somebody waiting in the wings. And remember that God's timing is always best. (Philippians 4:11-12)

3. **Be very choosy**: Don't "settle" for second-class treatment—you deserve someone who values you as a person . . . and shows it. (Psalm 40:1)

4. **Go to the right places**: If you want to meet new people, go to the places where you are likely to bump into the kind of people you want to meet: you probably won't find the right kind of person in the wrong kind of place. (1 Corinthians 15:33)

5. **Look beyond appearances**: Judging other people solely by appearances is tempting, but it's foolish, shortsighted, immature, and ultimately destructive. So don't do it. (Proverbs 16:22)

6: **Sex can wait**: If you're *really* serious about this guy, and if you're really serious about putting God first, then it's worth the wait.

7. **Trust God**: Your dating life, like every other aspect of your life, should glorify God; pray for His guidance, and follow it. (Proverbs 3:5-6)

Face the facts: being single and dating isn't all "fun and games." Dating can be stressful, very stressful. And remember that the choices you make in the dating world can have a profound impact on every other aspect of your life. So choose carefully and prayerfully.

Do not be unequally yoked together with unbelievers.
For what fellowship has righteousness with lawlessness?
And what communion has light with darkness?

2 CORINTHIANS 6:14 NKJV

A friend loves you all the time. . . .

PROVERBS 17:17 NCV

Beloved, if God so loved us, we also ought to love one another.

1 JOHN 4:11 NKJV

It is good and pleasant when God's people live together in peace!

PSALM 133:1 NCV

And may the Lord make you increase and abound in love
to one another and to all.

1 THESSALONIANS 3:12 NKJV

Sacrificial love, giving-up love, is love that is willing to go to any lengths to provide for the well-being of the beloved.

ED YOUNG

Only joyous love redeems.

CATHERINE MARSHALL

Love simply cannot spring up without that self-surrender to each other. If either withholds the self, love cannot exist.

E. STANLEY JONES

Live your lives in love, the same sort of love which Christ gives us, and which He perfectly expressed when He gave Himself as a sacrifice to God.

CORRIE TEN BOOM

ADDITIONAL BIBLE READINGS

PROVERBS 27:9; JOHN 15:13; 2 JOHN 1:3; AMOS 3:3;

SONG OF SOLOMON 2:16

EDUCATING YOUR CHILDREN

I f you're the mother of a young child, then you may be struggling with one of motherhood's most difficult dilemmas: how best to educate your child. Today, educational options are greater than ever before: public schools, private schools, home schools, on-line education—you and your child have choices that were unknown to previous generations. As you make choices about your child's education, consider the advice that follows:

Stress the importance of education: Make yours a home in which the importance of education is clearly a high priority.

Consider your options: Here in the 21st Century, you and your child have a wide range of educational options. Weigh those options carefully.

Be assertive: When it comes to educating your child, don't be satisfied to go with the flow. Instead, stand up and be counted . . . for your kid.

Invest in your child's educational tool kit: That tool kit should include books, arts and crafts materials, and a computer (with age-appropriate educational software), for starters.

Don't allow your child to become a slave to the TV: when it comes to the important task of filling your child's mind, reading beats watching.

Remember that it's your responsibility: Teachers will do their best, as will school administrators. But in the end, it's up to you to ensure that your child earns the benefits of a good education.

Remember that it's worth the cost: Face it—getting your kid through school is expensive in terms of time and money. But remember this: the value of a good education far outweighs its cost.

Wise mothers understand the value of education, but many children do not. Thus, the first lesson that a good parent must teach is the importance of education.

Education is the tool by which we come to know and appreciate the world in which we live. It is the shining light that snuffs out the darkness of ignorance and poverty. Education is freedom just as surely as ignorance is a form of bondage. Education is not a luxury, it is a necessity. And, when we prepare our youth with a firm foundation grounded in the basics of reading, writing, and mathematics, we prepare them for success . . . and we help provide for generations yet unborn.

*Therefore you shall lay up these words of mine in your heart and
in your soul . . . . You shall teach them to your children,
speaking of them when you sit in your house,
when you walk by the way, when you lie down,
and when you rise up.*

DEUTERONOMY 11:18-19 NKJV

*In every way be an example of doing good deeds.
When you teach, do it with honesty and seriousness.*

TITUS 2:7 NCV

*Correct your children while there is still hope;
do not let them destroy themselves.*

PROVERBS 19:18 NCV

*Train up a child in the way he should go,
and when he is old he will not depart from it.*

PROVERBS 22:6 NKJV

The mother is and must be, whether she knows it or not,
the greatest, strongest,
and most lasting teacher her children have.

HANNAH WHITALL SMITH

A child educated only at school is an undereducated child.

GEORGE SANTAYANA

Education is useless without the Bible.

NOAH WEBSTER

Enter school to learn; depart to serve.

MARY MCLEOD BETHUNE

ADDITIONAL BIBLE READINGS

3 JOHN 1:4; MATTHEW 18:5-6; 2 TIMOTHY 2:24; 2 TIMOTHY 3:14-15;

PROVERBS 20:7

TEENAGERS

Being a young adult in today's world isn't easy. Today's teenagers are confronted with temptations and distractions that were unknown to previous generations. And the world seems to be changing so rapidly at times that it's difficult for young people to make intelligent decisions.

In a society that is built upon the shifting sands of popular culture, God's laws remain constant. In a time of uncertainty and doubt, God's promises are sure and true. The solution, then, for the challenges of everyday living are found not in the trends of the moment but instead in the Word of God.

The teenage years can difficult, even for the most levelheaded kids. The following parenting tips can help you help your child:

Be massively involved: As a concerned parent, you should involve yourself, to the maximum extent possible, in the activities of your teenager.

Demand to know what's going on: When your youngster leaves the house, you should know where your child is going, and with whom. And you should also know when your child is expected to return home.

Insist on knowing your child's friends: Your teenager may want to keep his or her friends at a "safe" distance. But parental apathy is never the safest course of action. So do yourself and your child a favor: get to know those friends well, and don't apologize for doing so.

Talk things over: Even when certain conversations make you a little bit uncomfortable, keep talking. Your child needs your input, and even more importantly, your child needs to know that you care enough to give your input.

Listen with your ears and eyes: Wise mothers listen carefully to the things their youngsters say *and* to things their youngsters *don't* say.

Help your teenager understand that the media's messages are wrong: Many of the messages that stream from the media are specifically designed to sell your child products that interfere with his or her spiritual, physical, or emotional health. Help your child become a thoughtful consumer of the media's messages *and* the products that those messages are intended to sell.

Stress Safety: The teenage years can be dangerous years. As a concerned parent, you must help your teenager understand the need to behave responsibly.

---

*Have you not known? Have you not heard? The everlasting God,
the Lord, the Creator of the ends of the earth, neither faints nor
is weary. His understanding is unsearchable. He gives power to
the weak, and to those who have no might He increases strength.
Even the youths shall faint and be weary, and the young men shall
utterly fall, but those who wait on the Lord Shall renew their strength;
they shall mount up with wings like eagles, they shall run and
not be weary, they shall walk and not faint.*

ISAIAH 40:28–31 NKJV

*Be an example to the believers in word,
in conduct, in love, in spirit, in faith, in purity.*

1 TIMOTHY 4:12 NKJV

*How can a young person live a pure life?
By obeying your word.*

PSALM 119:9 NCV

*Blessed are those who hunger and thirst for righteousness,
for they shall be filled.*

MATTHEW 5:6 NKJV

The time for teaching and training is preteen.
When they reach the teenage years,
it's time to shut up and start listening.

RUTH BELL GRAHAM

There's a lot to be said for the compassion and
understanding that are gained when we've experienced
God's grace firsthand as a teenager.

LISA WHELCHEL

Pray for guidance; pray for strength; pray for patience, sanity,
and courage. And remember that God is big enough
to handle any problem . . . even teenagers.

MARIE T. FREEMAN

Parents can show respect as their teens begin to
express independence by allowing them to be
the unique individuals God made them to be.

TED ENGSTROM

ADDITIONAL BIBLE READINGS

ECCLESIASTES 12:1; 2 TIMOTHY 2:22; PSALM 103:5; COLOSSIANS 3:21;

PROVERBS 1:8-9; PROVERBS 13:24

MARITAL DIFFICULTIES

L ove is a journey—but not always an *easy* journey. A healthy marriage is a lifelong exercise in love, fidelity, trust, understanding, forgiveness, caring, sharing, and encouragement. It requires empathy, tenderness, patience, and perseverance. It is the union of two adults, both of whom are willing to compromise and, when appropriate, to apologize. It requires heaping helpings of common sense, common courtesy, and uncommon caring. A healthy marriage is a joy to behold, an even greater joy to experience…and a blessing forever.

The loving relationship between a husband and wife may require the couple to travel together through the dark valleys of disappointment and sorrow, but even on those darkest days, the couple can remain steadfast . . . if they choose to follow God.

No marriage is without problems. And, if you and your husband are encountering difficulties in your relationship, here are some things you should do:

Don't ignore problems: The issues that are ignored are the ones that take the longest to repair.

Trust God's Word: When you encounter difficulties within your marriage, God's Word should serve as a shining beacon.

Don't hesitate to ask for help. Don't hesitate to talk to your pastor or, if the circumstances warrant, to a marriage counselor.

Don't give up: Your marriage is worth working for . . . so keep working, keep smiling, and keep trusting that you and your spouse can make things better.

Keep praying: God answers prayers, but He's unlikely to answer the prayers that you forget to pray.

Are you and your spouse tired or troubled? Turn your hearts toward God in prayer. Are you weak or worried? Take the time—or, more accurately, make the time—to delve deeply into God's Holy Word. Are you spiritually depleted? Call upon fellow believers to support you, and call upon Christ to renew your marriage and your lives. When you do, you'll discover that the Creator of the universe stands ready to restore your strength, your relationship, and your love.

So then, they are no longer two but one flesh.
Therefore what God has joined together,
let not man separate.

MATTHEW 19:6 NKJV

Marriage should be honored by everyone,
and husband and wife should keep their marriage pure.

HEBREWS 13:4 NCV

A good wife is like a crown for her husband.

PROVERBS 12:4 NCV

Nevertheless let each one of you in particular
so love his own wife as himself,
and let the wife see that she respects her husband.

EPHESIANS 5:33 NKJV

Marriage is God's idea. He "crafted" it. If your marriage is broken, all the "repairmen" or counselors or seminars you take it to will be unable to fix it; take it to Him. The Creator Who made it in the first place can make it work again.

ANNE GRAHAM LOTZ

On the pleasant days of marriage, gaze across at your groom and conclude he is worth it. On the difficult days of marriage, gaze up at your Groom and conclude He's worth it.

BETH MOORE

Conflict can become either the source of greater intimacy or the source of greater isolation.

ED YOUNG

Those who abandon ship the first time it enters a storm miss the calm beyond. And the rougher the storms weathered together, the deeper and stronger real love grows.

RUTH BELL GRAHAM

ADDITIONAL BIBLE READINGS

GENESIS 2:24; COLOSSIANS 3:18-19; 1 CORINTHIANS 7:3; EPHESIANS 5:33; PROVERBS 18:22; PROVERBS 31:10; PROVERBS 31:30-31

MARRIAGE ENRICHMENT

W ho's in charge of your marriage? Is it you, is it your husband, or is it God? If you answered "God," then you've made the right choice. When you and your spouse build your marriage upon the transforming message of Jesus Christ, you're building on solid ground.

When you and your husband allow Christ to reign over your lives and your marriage, you will be transformed; you will feel differently about yourselves, your marriage, your family, and your world. The familiar words of John 10:10 promise that Jesus offers abundance to all who believe in Him: "I have come that they may have life, and that they may have it more abundantly" (NKJV). As believers who have been saved by a risen Christ, you and your husband should accept God's promise of spiritual abundance, and you should share that abundance with each other and the world.

Few things in life are more sad, or, for that matter, more absurd, than the sight of a grumpy Christian couple bickering about everything in sight. Don't ever be like that. God wants you to experience abundant, joyous relationships, but He expects you to do your fair share of the work. As you and your husband begin that work, here are some things that can help:

Faith first! The best marriages are built upon a shared faith in God. If yours is not, then you're building upon a foundation of sand.

Honor your spouse: Any marriage that doesn't honor God first and spouse second is destined for problems, and soon.

Be Cooperative: Remember that the two of you are "in this thing" together, so play like teammates, not rivals. (Matthew 12:25)

Forgive and Keep Forgiving: If you're having trouble forgiving your husband, think of all the times your husband has forgiven you! (1 Peter 4:8)

Be Encouraging: The words from the old cowboy song are familiar: "And seldom is heard a discouraging word . . . ." And if it's good enough for "Home on the Range," it's good enough for your home, too. Make certain that your little abode is a haven of encouragement for every member of your clan. You do so by checking your gripes and disappointments at the front door . . . and encouraging everybody else to do likewise! (Hebrews 3:13)

Be patient . . . *very* patient: Want him to be patient with you? Then you must do the same for him. (Proverbs 19:11)

Remember that honesty matters: Trust is important. If you want your marriage to flourish, you must be honest and trustworthy. (Proverbs 28:18)

Commitment, commitment, commitment! The best marriages are built upon an unwavering commitment to God and an unwavering commitment to one's spouse. So, if you're totally committed, congratulations; if you're not, you're building your marriage (and your life) on a very shaky foundation.

---

*Though I speak with the tongues of men and of angels,
but have not love, I have become sounding brass or
a clanging cymbal. And though I have the gift of prophecy,
and understand all mysteries and all knowledge, and
though I have all faith, so that I could remove mountains,
but have not love, I am nothing. And though I bestow
all my goods to feed the poor, and though I give my body
to be burned, but have not love, it profits me nothing.*

*Love suffers long and is kind; love does not envy;
love does not parade itself, is not puffed up;
does not behave rudely, does not seek its own, is not
provoked, thinks no evil; does not rejoice in iniquity,
but rejoices in the truth; bears all things, believes all things,
hopes all things, endures all things.*

Love never fails. But whether there are prophecies, they will fail; whether there are tongues, they will cease; whether there is knowledge, it will vanish away. For we know in part and we prophesy in part. But when that which is perfect has come, then that which is in part will be done away.

When I was a child, I spoke as a child, I understood as a child, I thought as a child; but when I became a man, I put away childish things. For now we see in a mirror, dimly, but then face to face. Now I know in part, but then I shall know just as I also am known. And now abide faith, hope, love, these three; but the greatest of these is love.

1 CORINTHIANS 13:1-13 NKJV

My commitment to my marriage vows places me in
an utterly unique and profoundly significant relationship
with the most important human being on earth—my spouse.

JONI EARECKSON TADA

As I grew older, I realized that my parents' love for one another
was deeper than just the look in their eyes each time one of
them came into the room. Their love was based on more than
their physical and emotional attraction. It was based on solid,
uncompromising commitment, first to Jesus Christ,
and second to the institution of marriage.

GIGI GRAHAM TCHIVIDJIAN

If the Living Logos of God has the power to create and
sustain the universe… He is more than able to sustain
your marriage and your ministry, your faith and your finances,
your hope and your health.

ANNE GRAHAM LOTZ

In the bond of marriage, we are to stand at the altar of Sacrifice
or we're not to stand at all.

BETH MOORE

ADDITIONAL BIBLE READINGS

EPHESIANS 5:33; MATTHEW 19:4-6; HEBREWS 13:4; EPHESIANS 4:26

SINGLE MOTHERHOOD

I f you're a single mom, then you already know the demands of your job are as relentless as they are rewarding. Yes, you know firsthand that being a single mom is a 24-7, 365-day-a-year profession. So what's a single mother to do? Here are a few things to consider:

If you're still mourning the loss of your spouse or the breakup of your marriage, be patient: you and your children may still need time to make the emotional adjustments that are necessary to really move on with your lives. But of this you can be sure: If you trust God and make genuine efforts to move on with your life, you will eventually be successful. (Psalm 125:1)

Be an active participant at church: the church needs you and, just as importantly, you and your children need the church. So, don't hesitate to lean upon your church for support. (1 Corinthians 3:9)

If you find yourself under growing financial pressure . . . face up to the realities of your situation right now. Then, begin taking whatever steps are necessary to put you and your family back on firm financial footing.

Don't be afraid (or embarrassed) to ask for help: people are willing to help *if* you ask . . . so ask! (Matthew 7:7-8)

Make time for yourself: Arrange your schedule so that you have at least a few minutes to yourself each day. Perhaps this means getting up a little earlier each morning (or staying up for a few minutes after the children have gone to bed). Even if it's difficult to find the time, you still need to spend time by yourself each day to collect your thoughts, prioritize your life, and talk with your God. (Isaiah 30:15)

Continue to invest in yourself: It's never too late to continue your education. Your future depends, to a very great extent, upon how much you are willing to invest in yourself. So keep learning and keep growing personally, professionally, and spiritually.

Talk to God early and often: One way to make sure that your heart is in tune with God is to pray often. The more you talk to God, the more He will talk to you.

And finally, remember this: God loves you . . . and if you're good enough for God, then shouldn't you be willing to love yourself, too? Of course you should!

Shepherd the flock of God which is among you.

1 PETER 5:2 NKJV

God has chosen you and made you his holy people.
He loves you. So always do these things: Show mercy to others,
be kind, humble, gentle, and patient.

COLOSSIANS 3:12 NCV

Unless the Lord builds the house,
They labor in vain who build it; Unless the Lord guards the city,
The watchman stays awake in vain.

PSALMS 127:1 NKJV

You must choose for yourselves today whom you will serve . . .
as for me and my family, we will serve the Lord.

JOSHUA 24:15 NCV

There is no influence so powerful as that of a mother.

SARAH J. HALE

All mothers are rich when they love their children.
There are no poor mothers, no old ones.
Their love is always the most beautiful of joys.

MAURICE MAETERLINCK

Maternal love: a miraculous substance which
God multiplies as he divides it.

VICTOR HUGO

Being a mother isn't my job; it's my life.

MARIE T. FREEMAN

ADDITIONAL BIBLE READINGS

DEUTERONOMY 6:6-9; PSALM127:3-5; JOSHUA 1:9

STAY-AT-HOME MOTHERHOOD

One stay-at-home mother described herself this way: "I'm just a mom." That's like saying, "I'm just an astronaut," or "I'm just a Supreme Court Justice." Motherhood is not *just* another job. It's one of the most important jobs in God's creation.

As a mother, you understand the critical importance of raising your children with love, with discipline, and with God. You know that your overriding purpose is to care for your children. And as you do so, here are some things to consider:

If you're a full-time, stay-at-home mom, you should place a high value your chosen career: You're never "just a mom." You're fulfilling one of the most important duties on planet earth . . . and don't ever forget it!

Make sure that your family's spiritual foundation is built upon "the rock": As a stay-at-home mom, you are, without question, your child's most important teacher. Make sure that your family's curriculum includes lots of lessons from the Bible.

Carve out time for yourself: It may seem like there's not a moment to spare . . . but it's up to you to make time for yourself—time to preserve your sanity to restore your soul.

Get plenty of rest: After you put your kids to bed, you should start thinking about going to bed, too. After all, *they're* going to wake up with lots of energy, and if you wake up groggy, you'll be overmatched!

Talk to other stay-at-home moms: Your challenges are not unique. By talking things over with other moms, you'll help yourself, and you'll help them, too.

Keep your husband informed and involved: As your partner, he deserves to know what's on your mind; he deserves to know how hard you work; he deserves to know how he can help; and he deserves to know much you appreciate his contribution.

Learn from the experts, but listen to your heart: After you're heard from all the "experts" trust that quiet inner voice that tells you right from wrong.

Pray about it! No problem is too great—or too small—for God. So pray.

Remember this: no family is perfect, and neither is yours—and it's perfectly okay to be imperfect. And, despite of the inevitable challenges of family life, your clan is God's gift to you. That little band of men, women, kids, and babies comprises a priceless treasure on temporary loan from the Father above. As you prayerfully seek God's direction, remember that He has important plans for you and your family. It's up to you, as a responsible mom, to act—and to plan—accordingly.

Then they can teach the young women to love their husbands, to love their children, to be wise and pure, to be good workers at home, to be kind . . . . Then no one will be able to criticize the teaching God gave us.

Titus 2:4-5 NCV

Choose for yourselves this day whom you will serve . . . .
But as for me and my house, we will serve the Lord.

JOSHUA 24:15 NKJV

Train up a child in the way he should go,
and when he is old he will not depart from it.

PROVERBS 22:6 NKJV

Correct your children while there is still hope;
do not let them destroy themselves.

PROVERBS 19:18 NCV

Her children rise up and call her blessed.

PROVERBS 31:28 NKJV

Being a full-time mom is the hardest job I've ever had,
but it is also the best job I've ever had.
The pay is lousy, but the rewards are eternal.

LISA WHELCHEL

The loveliest masterpiece of the heart of God is
the heart of a mother.

ST. THÉRÈSE OF LISIEUX

Mothers must model the tenderness we need.
Our world can't find it anywhere else.

CHARLES SWINDOLL

ADDITIONAL BIBLE READINGS

1 SAMUEL 1:27-28; PROVERBS 29:17; PSALM 128:1-3

WORKING MOMS

Nobody ever said that being a working mom was easy . . . and "nobody" was right! It's tough to hold down a job and raise a family at the same time—tough but not impossible.

If you're a working mom, then you know firsthand that motherhood isn't just the world's oldest profession, it's also the hardest! And as you work diligently to help make your child's life a masterpiece, here are some things to consider:

Strive for balance: Lots of people are clamoring for your attention, your time, and your energy. It's up to you to establish priorities that are important for you and your family. And remember, if you don't establish priorities, the world has a way of doing the job for you.

Learn to say "no": The word "no" is one of the greatest timesaving tools ever invented! Remember that you have a right to say "No" to requests that you consider unreasonable or inconvenient. Don't feel guilty for asserting your right to say "No," and don't feel compelled to fabricate excuses for your decisions.

Look for support, and keep looking until you find it . . . starting, of course, with your church.

Find time to exercise: it's the right thing to do, and you can find the time if you *really* want to.

Do whatever it takes to get enough sleep: Burning the candle at both ends isn't fun or smart. So turn off the TV, and go to bed as soon as possible after your children do. They need a good night's sleep, and so, for that matter, do you.

Find a workplace that is family friendly: Some companies are family-friendly, and some companies aren't. Make sure that you choose to work for an organization that understands—and appreciates—your role as a mom.

Get Organized: Every minute that you spend organizing your house can save ten minutes of effort later on. When it comes to managing a household, organization pays big dividends . . . and as a working mom, you deserve all the dividends you can get.

The plans of the diligent lead surely to plenty.

PROVERBS 21:5 NKJV

Whatever work you do, do your best,
because you are going to the grave,
where there is no working . . . .

ECCLESIASTES 9:10 NCV

And let the beauty of the Lord our God be upon us,
And establish the work of our hands for us;
Yes, establish the work of our hands.

PSALM 90:17 NKJV

Therefore by their fruits you will know them.

MATTHEW 7:20 NKJV

The unfolding of our friendship with the Father will be
a never-ending revelation stretching on into eternity.

CATHERINE MARSHALL

He stands fast as your rock, steadfast as your safeguard,
sleepless as your watcher, valiant as your champion.

C. H. SPURGEON

The Lord God of heaven and earth, the Almighty Creator of
all things, He who holds the universe in His hand as though
it were a very little thing, He is your Shepherd, and He has
charged Himself with the care and keeping of you, as a shepherd
is charged with the care and keeping of his sheep.

HANNAH WHITALL SMITH

No matter what we are going through, no matter how long
the waiting for answers, of one thing we may be sure. God is
faithful. He keeps His promises. What he starts, He finishes...
including His perfect work in us.

GLORIA GAITHER

ADDITIONAL BIBLE READINGS

PROVERBS 31:16-17; PROVERBS 31:21; PROVERBS 14:1

PART III

LEARNING HOW TO LIVE IN A DIFFICULT WORLD

This world can be a place of suffering and danger. But, as believers, we are comforted by the knowledge that God still sits in His heaven. He sees the grand scope of His creation, a vision that we, as mortals, cannot see. Even though we don't fully understand God's plans, we must trust His wisdom and His will, and we must seek to do His will here on earth.

In Part III of this text, we consider how best to live in this difficult world.

ABORTION

Although the numbers change from year to year, it is estimated that almost 900,000 abortions are performed each year in America. Since the Supreme Court made abortion legal in 1973, over 40,000,000 abortions have been performed here. As a consequence, millions of women continue to think about children who were never born. They ponder the consequences of their actions, and they ask themselves, "What if . . . "

If you've had an abortion—even if that abortion occurred many years ago—you may still have feelings of grief, or shame, or guilt, or all three. If so, you must remember this: the instant you ask God for His forgiveness, He gives it. So, if you've sincerely asked God to forgive, then you are forgiven . . . period. But sometimes forgiving *yourself* can be much harder. Why? Because (amazing as it seems) you're holding yourself to a higher standard

> **If you're thinking about having sex before marriage** . . . then you should also think long and hard about the options you will have *if* you become pregnant. The best time to think about adoption versus abortion is before you get the results of your pregnancy test, not after. And, if thinking about the choice between adoption and abortion leaves you with a sick feeling in the pit of your stomach, then don't have sex until you're fully prepared to keep your baby.

than God does! God's position on forgiveness is clear: if you ask for His forgiveness, and if you sincerely repent from your sinful behavior, He wipes the slate clean. You simply cannot "out-sin" God's ability to forgive.

If you're still grieving the consequences of an abortion, it is now time to take God at His word: you must open your heart to Him and accept His forgiveness once and for all. He is standing at the door of your heart, and He knocks. Will you answer Him? Prayerfully, you will . . . right now.

> **If you're unmarried and pregnant . . .** you may be encouraged to consider abortion as "the easy solution." But, God does not ask you to do the "easy" thing, He asks you to do the right thing, even when it's hard. And please remember that you have many more options than you might imagine . . . so *please* ask God to help you determine what those options are.

Come near to God, and God will come near to you.
You sinners, clean sin out of your lives. You who are trying to
follow God and the world at the same time, make your thinking pure.

JAMES 4:8 NCV

---

*If we say that we have no sin, we deceive ourselves,
and the truth is not in us. If we confess our sins,
He is faithful and just to forgive us our sins and to cleanse us
from all unrighteousness.*

1 JOHN 1:8-9 NKJV

*Now that you are obedient children of God do not live as you did
in the past. You did not understand, so you did the evil things
you wanted. But be holy in all you do, just as God,
the One who called you, is holy.*

1 PETER 1:14–15 NCV

*There is therefore now no condemnation to those who are in
Christ Jesus, who do not walk according to the flesh,
but according to the Spirit.*

ROMANS 8:1 NKJV

*He who covers his sins will not prosper,
but whoever confesses and forsakes them will have mercy.*

PROVERBS 28:13 NKJV

God's mercy is infinite, but it always flows to men through
the golden channel of Jesus Christ, his son.

C. H. SPURGEON

Mistakes offer the possibility for redemption and
a new start in God's kingdom. No matter what you're guilty of,
God can restore your innocence.

BARBARA JOHNSON

God knows my recklessness and sees my unfaithfulness,
and yet he stands with arms open wide to welcome me home.
God is the one who calls me back.

SHEILA WALSH

There is only One who can cleanse us from our sins—
He who made us.

CORRIE TEN BOOM

ADDITIONAL BIBLE READINGS

DEUTERONOMY 4:31; HEBREWS 4:16; JOHN 3:16; PSALM 103:17

ABUSIVE RELATIONSHIPS

If you lived in a perfect world, all your relationships would be uplifting, encouraging, empowering, and loving. But you don't live in a perfect world; you live in a world populated by decidedly imperfect people, and as a result, your relationships will be equally imperfect. On occasion, your relationships may become abusive, and when they do, it's time for you to stand up for yourself. And if you're a mother, it's time for you to take a stand for your children, too.

If you're involved in a troubling or abusive relationship, here's are some "do's and don'ts":

Consider safety to be an issue of the highest priority: If you're in an explosive relationship, you must protect yourself and your children. So do the wise thing—think "safety first": safety for yourself and safety for your family. (Proverbs 3:18)

Steadfastly refuse to think of yourself as a victim: Instead, think of yourself as a woman who needs to take action now—and think of yourself as a strong-willed woman who can take action! (James 1:22)

Do consider all your options: And remember this: If you think you don't have any options, you're not thinking clearly enough. (Luke 18:27)

Don't try to "change" the person who is abusing you: Trying to "reform" other people is usually futile; other people must reform themselves—and hopefully, with God's help, they will do so—but you cannot force them to do so. (Psalm 118:8-9)

Do look for help help: Whether you realize it or not, lot's of folks want to help you; let them. (Proverbs 11:25)

Don't abandon hope: Other people have experienced the same kind of hard times you may be experiencing now. They made it, and so can you. (Psalm 146:5)

A destructive relationship seldom starts out that way—in the beginning, the relationship may seem ideal, or nearly so. But over time, as the relationship gradually begins to deteriorate, small problems evolve into big troubles. So, if you find yourself in a relationship that is harmful to your health, your safety, or your sanity, don't be satisfied with the status quo. Pray for strength; pray for wisdom; pray for courage; and then, get busy creating a better world for you and yours.

> **Rape**: The Center for Disease Control calls rape "one of the most underreported crimes" in America. In fact, one study found that over 80% of rapes went unreported. Why? The answer stems, in part, from the fact that most rape victims *actually know their attackers*! If you've been assaulted, you may be tempted to do the "easy" thing, which is nothing. A better strategy is to do the hard work of confronting the reality of your attack, reporting your attacker, and beginning the difficult work of moving through and beyond the physical and psychological trauma that you've endured.

Don't make friends with quick-tempered people or spend time with those who have bad tempers. If you do, you will be like them. Then you will be in real danger.

PROVERBS 22:24-25 NCV

Don't become angry quickly, because getting angry is foolish.

ECCLESIASTES 7:9 NCV

My dear brothers and sisters, always be willing to listen and slow to speak. Do not become angry easily, because anger will not help you live the right kind of life God wants.

JAMES 1:19-20 NCV

Be strong and of good courage, and do it; do not fear nor be dismayed, for the Lord God—my God—will be with you. He will not leave you nor forsake you, until you have finished all the work for the service of the house of the Lord.

1 CHRONICLES 28:20 NKJV

When something robs you of your peace of mind, ask yourself
if it is worth the energy you are expending on it.
If not, then put it out of your mind in an act of discipline.
Every time the thought of "it" returns, refuse it.

KAY ARTHUR

Some folks cause happiness wherever
they go, others whenever they go.

BARBARA JOHNSON

You don't have to attend every argument you're invited to!

ANONYMOUS

A man wrapped up in himself makes a very small package.

BEN FRANKLIN

ADDITIONAL BIBLE READINGS

PROVERBS 16:32; PROVERBS 19:11; PROVERBS 29:22; JAMES 3:17

ADDICTION

You live in an addictive society. The supply of addictive substances continues to grow; the affordability and availability of these substances makes them highly attractive to consumers; and the effort to sell you these substances is relentless.

The list of addictive products is extensive: alcohol, drugs (illegal and prescription varieties), cigarettes, gambling (often government-sponsored), sex (an age-old profession with a new twist: on-line pornography), and food (100 years ago, overeating would not have qualified as a major addiction, but oh how things have changed).

The dictionary defines addiction as "the compulsive need for a habit-forming substance; the condition of being habitually and compulsively occupied with something." That definition is accurate, but incomplete. For Christians, addiction has an additional meaning: it means compulsively worshipping something other than God. And, unless you're living on a deserted island, you know people who are full-blown addicts—probably lots of people. If you, or someone you love, is suffering from the blight of addiction, here are a few things to consider:

For the addict, God does not come first; the addiction comes first. In the life of an addict, addiction rules. God, of course, commands otherwise. God says, "You shall have no other gods before Me," and He means precisely what He says (Exodus 20:3 NKJV). Our task, as believers, is to put God in His proper place: first place.

Help is available: Lots of people have experienced addiction and lived to tell about it. They want to help. Let them. (Proverbs 27:17)

Try though you might, you simply cannot cure another person's addiction. What you can do is to encourage the addicted person to seek help. The cure for addiction begins when the addict sincerely decides to seek treatment, not when you decide to seek treatment. So, instead of taking responsibility for curing the addict, you should be supportive by encouraging that person to find the help that he or she needs. (Luke 10:25-37)

> **Internet Pornography:**
> Internet users beware: viewing pornography on the Internet can be highly addictive. Parents must protect their children from this blight, and adults must protect themselves . . . or suffer the terrifying consequences.

If you are living with an addicted person, think about safety: yours and your family's. Addiction is life-threatening and life-shortening. Don't let someone else's addiction threaten your safety or the safety of your loved ones. (Proverbs 22:3)

Don't become an enabler: When you interfere with the negative consequences that might otherwise accompany an addict's negative behaviors, you are inadvertently "enabling" the addict to continue the destructive cycle of addiction. Don't do it. (Proverbs 15:31)

Don't give up hope. A cure is possible. With God's help, no addiction is incurable. And with God, no situation is hopeless. (Matthew 19:26)

The Lord knows how to deliver the godly out of temptations.

2 PETER 2:9 NKJV

*For we do not have a High Priest who cannot sympathize with
our weaknesses, but was in all points tempted as we are,
yet without sin. Let us therefore come boldly to the throne of grace,
that we may obtain mercy and find grace to help in time of need.*

HEBREWS 4:15-16 NKJV

*Therefore submit to God. Resist the devil and he will flee from you.
Draw near to God and He will draw near to you.
Cleanse your hands, you sinners; and purify your hearts,
you double-minded.*

JAMES 4:7-8 NKJV

*Now the Lord is the Spirit; and where the Spirit of the Lord is,
there is liberty.*

2 CORINTHIANS 3:17 NKJV

And you shall know the truth, and the truth shall make you free.

JOHN 8:32 NKJV

Addiction is the most powerful psychic enemy of
humanity's desire for God.

GERALD MAY

We are meant to be addicted to God,
but we develop secondary additions that temporarily appear
to fix our problem.

EDWARD M. BERCKMAN

I pray God will open the eyes of women everywhere to
the Liberator Who has given His life to set them free
from spiritual, social, and psychological bondage.

ANNE GRAHAM LOTZ

Freedom is not the right to do what we want
but the power to do what we ought.

CORRIE TEN BOOM

ADDITIONAL BIBLE READINGS

PROVERBS 5:23; JAMES 5:19-20; 2 PETER 2:9; 1 PETER 5:8

COPING WITH CHANGE

As a woman making her way through the maze of 21st-Century life, you know from firsthand experience that the world is constantly changing. God, on the other hand, does not change. His Word promises, "I am the Lord, I do not change" (Malachi 3:6 NKJV).

Every day of your life, you will encounter a multitude of changes—some good, some not so good, some downright disheartening. On those occasions when you must endure life-changing personal losses that leave you reeling, there is a place you can turn for comfort and assurance—you can turn to God. When you do, your loving Heavenly Father stands ready to protect you, to comfort you, to guide you, and, in time, to heal you.

Some of your most important dreams will be the ones you abandon. Some of your most important goals will be the ones you don't attain. Sometimes, your most important journeys are the ones that will take you to the winding conclusion of what seems to be to be a dead end street. But with God there are no dead ends; there are only opportunities to learn, to yield, to trust, to serve, and to grow.

The next time you experience one of life's inevitable disappointments, don't despair and don't be afraid to try "Plan B." Consider every setback an opportunity to choose a different, more appropriate path. Have faith that God may indeed be leading you in an entirely different direction, a direction of His choosing. And as you take your next step, remember that what looks like a dead end to you may, in fact, be the fast lane according to God.

Have you encountered difficult circumstances or unwelcome changes? If so, please remember that God is far bigger than any problem you may face. So, instead of worrying about life's inevitable challenges, put your faith in the Father and His only begotten Son: "Jesus Christ is the same yesterday, today, and forever" (Hebrews 13:8 NKJV). And remember: it is precisely because your Savior does not change that you can face your challenges with courage for today and hope for tomorrow.

Does your corner of the world seem to be trembling beneath your feet? If so, seek protection from the One who cannot be moved. The same God who created the universe will protect you if you ask Him . . . so ask Him . . . and then serve Him with willing hands and a trusting heart.

*To everything there is a season,
a time for every purpose under heaven*

ECCLESIASTES 3:1 NKJV

*John said, "Change your hearts and lives
because the kingdom of heaven is near."*

MATTHEW 3:2 NCV

*So don't worry about tomorrow,
because tomorrow will have its own worries.
Each day has enough trouble of its own.*

MATTHEW 6:34 NCV

With God, it isn't who you were that matters;
it's who you are becoming.

LIZ CURTIS HIGGS

If God has you in the palm of his hand and your real life is
secure in him, then you can venture forth—
into the places and relationships, the challenges,
the very heart of the storm—and you will be safe there.

PAULA RINEHART

Let nothing disturb you, nothing frighten you;
all things are passing; God never changes.

ST. TERESA OF AVILA

We do not love each other without changing each other.
We do not observe the world around us without in some way
changing it, and being changed ourselves.

MADELEINE L'ENGLE

ADDITIONAL BIBLE READINGS

1 CORINTHIANS 15:51–57; MALACHI 3:6; MATTHEW 18:3-4; PROVERBS 27:12

BEING SINGLE

The single life . . . these three words mean different things to different people. Paul had great praise for the single life, but only for those people who have the internal fortitude to remain unmarried *and* celibate (1 Corinthians 7:8).

Being single has its own sets of challenges and rewards. And for many Christian women, the single life is a wonderful, comfortable existence.

So, whether you are happily single, permanently single, or single-but-looking, remember that God's hand is continuing to guide your life. Your task is to seek His guidance and to follow it. And while you're at it, consider the following advice.

Remember that God put you here for a reason . . . and He has important work for you to do, whether you're married or not.

Every experience in your life helps prepare you for the person you will be today and the person you will become tomorrow . . . and your experiences may be preparing you for the man you will meet today or tomorrow.

Don't feel compelled to date "just for the sake of dating." Sometimes dating can be fun, and sometimes dating can be painful. If you're not dating anybody at the moment, don't worry. It's better to be dating *nobody* than to be dating the wrong person.

Don't presume that being married is "right" and being single is "wrong": God has a plan for you that may include marriage or not. Your challenge is to obey God's Word and to follow in the footsteps of God's Son. If you do these things, God will handle the rest.

Keep God first in your life . . . and make sure that any man you invite into your life is willing to do the same.

Be patient: Waiting faithfully for God's plan to unfold is more important than understanding God's plan. Ruth Bell Graham once said, "When I am dealing with an all-powerful, all-knowing God, I, as a mere mortal, must offer my petitions not only with persistence, but also with patience. Someday I'll know why." Even when you can't understand God's plans, you must trust Him and never lose faith!

I will instruct you and teach you in the way you should go;
I will guide you with My eye.

PSALM 32:8 NKJV

In all your ways acknowledge Him,
and He shall direct your paths.

PROVERBS 3:6 NKJV

The true children of God are those who let
God's Spirit lead them.

ROMANS 8:14 NCV

I will lift up my eyes to the hills.
From whence comes my help? My help comes from the Lord,
Who made heaven and earth.

PSALM 121:1-2 NKJV

More God's Word About . . . RESPECTING YOURSELF

For You formed my inward parts; You covered me in my mother's womb. I will praise You, for I am fearfully and wonderfully made; Marvelous are Your works.

PSALM 139:13-14 NKJV

God began doing a good work in you, and I am sure he will continue it until it is finished when Jesus Christ comes again.

PHILIPPIANS 1:6 NCV

Your beliefs about these things should be kept secret between you and God. People are happy if they can do what they think is right without feeling guilty.

ROMANS 14:22 NCV

May He grant you according to your heart's desire, and fulfill all your purpose.

PSALM 20:4 NKJV

ADDITIONAL BIBLE READINGS

1 CORINTHIANS 7:7-8; PHILIPPIANS 4:11; PROVERBS 4:7; PROVERBS 4:23

DISCRIMINATION AT WORK

Although women have made tremendous strides in the workplace, discrimination still occurs. In far too many organizations, the "old boy network" still determines who is invited onto the "fast track." Oftentimes, women are viewed as being qualified for supporting roles in the organization, but not for starring roles. Such treatment is obviously unfair, but still commonplace.

If you're working at a job where you are not treated fairly, the worst thing you can no is nothing. Instead, make your feelings known to people who are willing to listen and willing to help. And if you don't see changes in a hurry, start searching for a new job immediately . . . and don't stop searching until you find it.

TIPS FOR THE WORKPLACE

If a coworker behaves inappropriately toward you, stand up for yourself. And if the behavior continues, speak directly to your supervisor.

Don't "settle" for any old job; keep searching for the right job. And while you're at it, keep improving your skills along the way.

If you feel that your rights are being violated in ways that are clearly illegal . . . talk things over with people you trust, starting with knowledgeable friends *and* with your pastor.

If you're uncertain of your next step, pray about it . . . and keep praying about it. You've got questions? God has answers.

Listen to your heart: In your heart, you know whether or not your current job is right for you. If things aren't working out, then your most important job is to find a new job.

Be of good courage, And He shall strengthen your heart,
All you who hope in the Lord.

PSALM 31:24 NKJV

And whatever you do, do it heartily, as to the Lord and not to men.

COLOSSIANS 3:23 NKJV

Do all you can to live a peaceful life.
Take care of your own business, and do your own work
as we have already told you.
If you do, then people who are not believers will respect you,
and you will not have to depend on others for what you need.

1 THESSALONIANS 4:11-12 NCV

"Be strong and brave, and do the work.
Don't be afraid or discouraged, because the Lord God, my God,
is with you. He will not fail you or leave you."

1 CHRONICLES 28:20 NCV

A person who doesn't work hard is just like
someone who destroys things.

PROVERBS 18:9 NCV

Thank God every morning when you get up that
you have something which must be done,
whether you like it or not.
Work breeds a hundred virtues
that idleness never knows.

CHARLES KINGSLEY

Working in the vineyard,
Working all the day,
Never be discouraged,
Only watch and pray.

FANNY CROSBY

Whatever I do, I give up my whole self to it.

EDNA ST. VINCENT MILLAY

ADDITIONAL BIBLE READINGS

1 CORINTHIANS 15:57-58; 1 CORINTHIANS 3:8; ROMANS 12:10-12;

LUKE 20:21; GALATIANS 2:6; JAMES 3:17

DIVORCE

There's really no way to get around the fact that Bible does not endorse divorce. In fact, the opposite is true: the Bible discourages divorce, and if we're to be obedient servants, so should we.

Jesus clearly teaches that divorce is wrong: "If a man divorces his wife and marries another woman, he is guilty of adultery, and the man who marries a divorced woman is also guilty of adultery" (Luke 16:18 NCV). And if that weren't clear enough, Jesus makes His point again with these familiar words: "Therefore what God has joined together, let no man separate" (Matthew 19:6 NKJV). So there you have it: divorce is an affront to God's Word. Period. But we live in a world where divorce is an ever-present reality that touches countless families. So what are divorced people to do? The answer is straightforward: to ask God's forgiveness for any past failings, to "sin no more" (John 8:10-11), and to seek, from this day forward, to live a life that is pleasing to Him.

If you are a divorced person, you may be experiencing a wide range of emotions: anger, pain, guilt, fear, and heartbreak, to name but a few. But even if you're struggling through the most difficult transition of your life, you must never lose faith. God remains faithful, and He's as near as your next heartbeat. As you turn to Him for guidance and support, here are a few things to consider:

God doesn't love divorce, but He still loves you. It's certainly no secret: the Bible teaches that divorce is wrong. Yet we must remember that ours is a merciful and a loving God. God loves you despite your shortcomings, and He loves you despite your divorce. (Romans 8:38-39)

God forgives sin when you ask . . . so ask! God stands ready to forgive . . . the next move is yours. (Psalm 51:1-2; James 5:11; Acts 10:43)

Bitterness is poison. If you continue to harbor feelings of bitterness or regret, it's time to forgive everybody (including yourself). If you are unable to forgive, ask God to help you, and keep asking Him until He removes the poison of bitterness from your heart. (Matthew 6:14-15; Matthew 7:7-8)

The past is past . . . so don't live there. If you're focused on the past, change your focus. If you're living in the past, it's time to stop living there. (Isaiah 43:18-19)

Sometimes, the greatest learning experiences are the ones that hurt the most. If you're divorced, you can—and should—learn from your experience. If you last relationship was troublesome—or worse—learn from it, so that your next relationship won't be. (Proverbs 21:11)

God is always near . . . and if you draw close to Him, He will draw close to you. (James 4:8)

After your divorce, God still has a wonderful plan for your life. And the time to start looking for that plan—and living it—is now. (Psalm 16:11)

Every misfortune, every failure, every loss may be transformed. God has the power to transform all misfortunes into "God-sends."

MRS. CHARLES E. COWMAN

Let us, then, feel very sure that we can come before God's throne where there is grace. There we can receive mercy and grace to help us when we need it.

HEBREWS 4:16 NCV

*For I am persuaded that neither death nor life,
nor angels nor principalities nor powers,
nor things present nor things to come, nor height nor depth,
nor any other created thing, shall be able to separate us from
the love of God which is in Christ Jesus our Lord.*

ROMANS 8:38-39 NKJV

*But God's mercy is great, and he loved us very much.
Though we were spiritually dead because of the things
we did against God, he gave us new life with Christ.
You have been saved by God's grace.*

EPHESIANS 2:4-5 NCV

*For if you forgive men their trespasses,
your heavenly Father will also forgive you.
But if you do not forgive men their trespasses,
neither will your Father forgive your trespasses.*

MATTHEW 6:14-15 NKJV

When trials come your way—as inevitably they will—
do not run away. Run to your God and Father.

KAY ARTHUR

There is no elation equal to the rise of the spirit to meet and
overcome a difficulty, not with a foolish overconfidence,
but by keeping things in their proper relations by praying,
now and then, the prayer of a good fighter whom I used to know;
"Lord, make me sufficient to mine own occasion."

LAURA INGALLS WILDER

God helps those who help themselves, but there are times
when we are quite incapable of helping ourselves.
That's when God stoops down and gathers us in His arms
like a mother lifts a sick child, and does for us
what we cannot do for ourselves.

RUTH BELL GRAHAM

ADDITIONAL BIBLE READINGS

LUKE 16:18; MALACHI 2:13–16; JOEL 2:25; EPHESIANS 5:21-33

THE EMPTY NEST

Much has been written about parents' responses to "the empty nest." When the last of the kids has moved out of the house, what's a mom to do? The answer, of course, is that God still has *plenty* of things for mom to do.

If you're an empty-nester, then you know the mixture of relief and sadness that may fill your heart when the last of your precious little chicks flies away from the nest. But even if your heart is heavy, you must never lose sight of this fact: God has important work for you to do, and He wants you to do that work sooner rather than later.

Proverbs 3:6 gives you guidance: "In all your ways acknowledge Him, and He shall direct your paths." When you think about it, the words in this verse make a powerful promise: If you acknowledge God's sovereignty over every aspect of your life, He will guide your path. That's an important promise. So, as you prayerfully consider the path that God intends for you to take, here are things you should do:

- You should study His Word and be ever-watchful for His signs.

- You should associate with fellow believers who will encourage your spiritual growth.

- You should listen carefully to that inner voice that speaks to you in the quiet moments of your daily devotionals.

- And, as you continually seek God's unfolding purpose for your life, you should be patient.

Your Heavenly Father may not always reveal Himself as quickly as you would like. But rest assured: God is sovereign, God is here, God is love, and God intends to use you in wonderful, unexpected ways. He desires to lead you along a path of His choosing. Your challenge is to watch, to listen, to learn . . . and to follow.

The eyes of the Lord are in every place, keeping watch . . . .

PROVERBS 15:3 NKJV

Have I not commanded you? Be strong and of good courage;
do not be afraid, nor be dismayed,
for the Lord your God is with you wherever you go.

JOSHUA 1:9 NKJV

Come near to God, and God will come near to you.

JAMES 4:8 NCV

Praise be to the God and Father of our Lord Jesus Christ.
God is the Father who is full of mercy and all comfort.
He comforts us every time we have trouble,
so when others have trouble, we can comfort them with
the same comfort God gives us.

2 CORINTHIANS 1:3–4 NCV

To adore is to be drawn away from my own preoccupations and into the presence of Jesus. It means letting go of what I want, what I desire, and what I have planned; it means fully trusting Jesus and his love.

HENRI NOUWEN

In the kingdom of God, the surest way to lose something is to try to protect it, and the best way to keep it is to let it go.

A. W. TOZER

Letting God have His way can be an uncomfortable thing.

CHARLES SWINDOLL

With each new experience of letting God be in control, we gain courage and reinforcement for daring to do it again and again.

GLORIA GAITHER

ADDITIONAL BIBLE READINGS

PSALM 24:1; PSALM 16:11; 2 CHRONICLES 16:9; LAMENTATIONS 3:24;

HEBREWS 13:5; JOHN 14:18

FINANCIAL STRESS

God's Word is not only a roadmap to eternal life, it is also an indispensable guidebook for life here on earth. As such, the Bible has much to say about your life and your finances.

The quest for financial security is a journey that leads us across many peaks and through a few unexpected valleys. When we celebrate life's great victories, we find it easy to praise God and to give thanks. But, when we find ourselves in the dark valleys of life, when we face disappointments or financial hardships, it's much more difficult to trust God's perfect plan. But, trust Him we must.

Will regular readings of your Bible make you a financial genius? Probably not. The Bible is God's Holy Word; it is intended not as a tool for prosperity, but as a tool for salvation. Nevertheless, the Bible can teach you how to become a more disciplined, patient person. As you become a more disciplined person in other aspects of your life, you will also become more disciplined in the management of your personal finances—and the following common-sense tips can help:

Enhance your earning power and keep enhancing your earning power: Opportunities to learn are limitless, and change is inevitable. In today's competitive workplace, those who stand still are, in reality, moving backwards . . . fast. (Proverbs 28:19)

Live within your means: Save money from every paycheck. Never spend more than you make. (Ecclesiastes 5:1)

Use credit wisely: Don't borrow money for things that rapidly go down in value (furniture, clothes, new cars, boats, etc.) And if you borrow money for things that are likely to go up (like your home), borrow only the amount that you can comfortably afford to repay (in other words, don't "max out" your mortgage!) (Proverbs 22:7)

Don't buy impulsively: Savvy salespeople want you to buy "right now." But savvy buyers take their time. (Proverbs 21:5)

Don't fall in love with "stuff." We live in a society that worships "stuff"—don't fall into that trap. Remember this: "stuff" is highly overrated. Worship God almighty, not the almighty dollar. (Proverbs 11:28)

Make sure that everybody in your family understands financial common sense. Within families, financial security is a team sport; make sure that everybody is on the team. (Matthew 12:25)

Give back to the Lord: God is the giver of all things good. What does He ask in return? A tiny ten percent. Don't withhold it from Him. (Malachi 3:10)

---

*And my God shall supply all your need according
to His riches in glory by Christ Jesus.*

PHILIPPIANS 4:19 NKJV

*Honor the Lord with your wealth and the firstfruits from
all your crops. Then your barns will be full,
and your wine barrels will overflow with new wine.*

PROVERBS 3:9-10 NCV

*Wise people's houses are full of the best foods and olive oil,
but fools waste everything they have.*

PROVERBS 21:20 NCV

*She watches over the ways of her household,
And does not eat the bread of idleness.*

PROVERBS 31:27 NKJV

Money is a mirror that, strange as it sounds,
reflects our personal weaknesses and strengths
with amazing clarity.

DAVE RAMSEY

Christians cannot experience peace in the area of finances
until they have surrendered total control of this area to God
and accepted their position as stewards.

LARRY BURKETT

If a Christian is worried, frustrated, and upset about money,
God is *not* in control.

LARRY BURKETT

ADDITIONAL BIBLE READINGS

2 CORINTHIANS 9:6; MATTHEW 25:21; PROVERBS 10:4; LUKE 6:38;

MALACHI 3:10; MATTHEW 6:31-33; PSALM 23:1; PSALM 34:9-10

HOMOSEXUALITY

We live in a society that, in a strange twist of fate, has come to glorify the practice of homosexuality. Gay marriage has been embraced by high-level, high-profile politicians. Gay-friendly television shows extol the keen observational powers of "the queer eye" (whatever that is). And remarkably, in one public television series aimed at young children, an episode addressed the lifestyle issues of a lesbian couple . . . in an animated cartoon intended for first-graders! This begs the question: where does "open-mindedness" stop and open rebellion against God begin?

The Bible clearly defines homosexuality as a sin (Leviticus 18:22). Most certainly it is not *the only* sin, nor is it an *unforgivable* sin—but it remains a sin nonetheless. So we should not take homosexuality lightly, nor should we trivialize it by making gay people objects of derision, curiosity, aggression, or humor.

In a letter to believers, Peter offers a stern warning: "Your adversary, the devil, walks about like a roaring lion, seeking whom he may devour" (I Peter 5:8 NKJV). What was true in New Testament times is equally true in our own. Satan tempts his prey and then devours them. As believing Christians, we must beware. And, if we seek righteousness in our own lives, we must earnestly wrap ourselves in the protection of God's Holy Word. When we do, we are secure.

*If we say that we have no sin, we deceive ourselves,
and the truth is not in us. If we confess our sins,
He is faithful and just to forgive us our sins and
to cleanse us from all unrighteousness.*

1 JOHN 1:8-9 NKJV

*Test all things; hold fast what is good.
Abstain from every form of evil.*

1 THESSALONIANS 5:21-22 NKJV

*We have around us many people whose lives tell us what faith means.
So let us run the race that is before us and never give up.
We should remove from our lives anything that would get in the way
and the sin that so easily holds us back.*

HEBREWS 12:1 NCV

*Put on the whole armor of God, that you may be able to
stand against the wiles of the devil.*

EPHESIANS 6:11 NKJV

In this is love, not that we loved God, but that He loved us and sent His Son to be the propitiation for our sins.

1 JOHN 4:10 NKJV

Yes, if you forgive others for their sins, your Father in heaven will also forgive you for your sins. But if you don't forgive others, your Father in heaven will not forgive your sins.

MATTHEW 6:14-15 NCV

All the prophets say it is true that all who believe in Jesus will be forgiven of their sins through Jesus' name.

ACTS 10:43 NCV

You have been born again, and this new life did not come from something that dies, but from something that cannot die. You were born again through God's living message that continues forever.

2 PETER 1:23 NCV

Too many Christians have geared their program to please,
to entertain, and to gain favor from this world.
We are concerned with how much, instead of how little,
like this age we can become.

BILLY GRAHAM

Our fight is not against any physical enemy;
it is against organizations and powers that are spiritual.
We must struggle against sin all our lives,
but we are assured we will win.

CORRIE TEN BOOM

Our soul can never have rest in things that are beneath itself.

JULIANA OF NORWICH

All those who look to draw their satisfaction from the wells of
the world—pleasure, popularity, position, possessions, politics,
power, prestige, finances, family, friends, fame, fortune, career,
children, church, clubs, sports, sex, success, recognition,
reputation, religion, education, entertainment, exercise,
honors, health, hobbies—will soon be thirsty again!

ANNE GRAHAM LOTZ

ADDITIONAL BIBLE READINGS

LEVITICUS 18:22; LEVITICUS 20:13; ROMANS 1:27;

I CORINTHIANS 6:9-10

INFIDELITY

Although accurate statistics on marital infidelity are notoriously difficult to compile (for obvious reasons), some estimates indicate that approximately 15% of wives and 25% of husbands have broken their marriage vows by engaging in extramarital sex. These estimates are probably somewhat *lower* than the actual percentages because in self-reporting surveys, infidelity is almost always underreported (again, for obvious reasons). Yet even if these statistics are *remotely* accurate, we can see that millions of families are being torn apart by an epidemic of infidelity that shows no signs of abating.

Infidelity is nothing new, but the nature 21st-century society seems to make it easier than ever. Experts describe a new "crisis of infidelity" that has come as a result of "platonic" friendships which usually begin in the workplace or on the Internet. These "friendships," which may seem harmless to the parties involved, can result in powerful physical and emotional attractions— attractions that can lead to infidelity. Godly husbands and wives must beware.

It's worth noting that infidelity comes in many shapes and sizes. A broader (and more useful) definition of marital infidelity should include *all* sexually motivated activities that 1. Create emotional distance between and husband and wife and 2. Require secrecy and deception on the part of one spouse. Thus, clandestine viewing of pornography, or the secret participation in sexually explicit Internet "chats" should be viewed as variant forms of infidelity, even though actual sexual contact between two adults has not occurred.

If you marriage has been torn apart by infidelity, here are some things to remember:

- God abhors marital infidelity, and He judges those harshly who break their marriage vows.

- If you begin to feel a strong temptation to break your marriage vows, you must:

  1. Distance yourself from the person to whom you feel attracted (even if that means changing jobs).
  2. Pray to God for the wisdom and the strength to resist the temptations that you feel.
  3. Make a strong effort to reconnect physically, spiritually, and emotionally with your spouse.

- If your husband has been guilty of infidelity, you must be willing to forgive him (even though you will never be able to forget his actions). However, if your husband is unwilling to repent from his adulterous behavior and return to your marriage, then you must prayerfully consider *all* your options while prayerfully considering the best interests of your children.

Marriage is honorable among all, and the bed undefiled;
but fornicators and adulterers God will judge.

HEBREWS 13:4 NKJV

For the Lord knows the way of the righteous,
but the way of the ungodly shall perish.

PSALM 1:6 NKJV

Whoever commits adultery with a woman lacks understanding;
He who does so destroys his own soul.

PROVERBS 6:32 NKJV

Therefore do not let sin reign in your mortal body,
that you should obey it in its lusts.

ROMANS 6:12 NKJV

Addiction and infidelity: Addiction and infidelity are traveling companions. If an intoxicating substance becomes your best friend, then you're inviting Old Man Trouble to your house for an extended stay. When you're under the grip of addictive substances, your reasoning powers are impaired. That's one reason—but not the only reason—that you must fight the curse of addiction with all the strength you can muster.

The greatest gift you can give your marriage partner is
your fidelity. The greatest character trait you can provide
your spouse and your family is moral and ethical self-control.

CHARLES SWINDOLL

Nothing is more noble, nothing more venerable than fidelity.
Faithfulness and truth are the most sacred excellences and
endowments of the human mind.

CICERO

The love life of the Christian is a crucial battleground.
There, if nowhere else, it will be determined who is Lord:
the world, the self, and the devil—or the Lord Christ.

ELISABETH ELLIOT

Marital love is a committed act of the will before it is
anything else. It is sacrificial love, a no-turning-back decision.

ED YOUNG

ADDITIONAL BIBLE READINGS

EXODUS 20:14; MATTHEW 5:27-28; MATTHEW 19:5-7; MALACHI 2:13-15;

PROVERBS 5:21-23

JOB LOSS

L osing your job can be an unsettling experience. Job loss can cause problems of the first magnitude, problems that result in financial and emotional stress. But there is indeed a lining around almost every cloud, and of this you can be sure: hidden beneath every lost job is the seed of a solution—God's solution. Your challenge, as a woman who honors God, is to trust God's providence and seek His solutions. When you do, you eventually discover that God does nothing without a very good reason: His reason.

If you've recently experienced a job loss, here are some things to consider and some things to do:

Take time to catch your breath . . . but not too much time. If you don't have a job, then your most important job is finding a new job. So don't sit around the house feeling sorry for yourself—get busy searching for your next employment opportunity.

Remember that God is still here: He rules the mountaintops of life and the valleys, so don't lose hope. (Lamentations 3:25-26)

If you're feeling sorry for yourself, stop: Self-pity isn't going to help you find a better job or build a better life. (2 Timothy 1:7)

Use all available tools. Those tools include, but are not limited to, friends, family, church members, former business associates, classified advertisements, employment services, the Internet, and your own shoe leather. (2 Peter 1:5-6)

Finding a new job is full-time work. If you need a new job, you should spend at least 40 hours a week looking for it. And you should keep doing so until you find the job you need. (1 Chronicles 28:20)

Be a Realistic Optimist: Your attitude toward the future will help create your future. You might as well put the self-fulfilling prophecy to work for you, and besides, life is far too short to be a pessimist. (Philippians 4:8)

Come to Me, all you who labor and are heavy laden,
and I will give you rest. Take My yoke upon you and learn from Me,
for I am gentle and lowly in heart, and you will find rest for
your souls. For My yoke is easy and My burden is light.

MATTHEW 11:28-30 NKJV

Through the Lord's mercies we are not consumed,
because His compassions fail not. They are new every morning;
Great is Your faithfulness.

LAMENTATIONS 3:22-23 NKJV

Be humble under God's powerful hand so he will lift you up
when the right time comes. Give all your worries to him,
because he cares about you.

1 PETER 5:6-7 NCV

Peace I leave with you, My peace I give to you;
not as the world gives do I give to you.
Let not your heart be troubled, neither let it be afraid.

JOHN 14:27 NKJV

Snuggle in God's arms. When you are hurting,
when you feel lonely or left out,
let Him cradle you, comfort you,
reassure you of His all-sufficient power and love.

KAY ARTHUR

The Lord is the one who travels every mile of
the wilderness way as our leader, cheering us,
supporting and supplying and fortifying us.

ELISABETH ELLIOT

God is always sufficient in perfect proportion to our need.

BETH MOORE

ADDITIONAL BIBLE READINGS

2 SAMUEL 22:2-3; 1 CHRONICLES 28:20; PSALM 31:14-15;

PSALM 62:8

LONELINESS

If you're like most women, you've experienced occasional bouts of loneliness. If so, you understand the psychological pain that accompanies those feelings that "nobody cares." Of course, the real facts are seldom as desperate as you imagine them to be. In actuality, many people care about you, but at times, you may hardly notice their presence.

Sometimes, feelings of profound loneliness may be the result of untreated depression; in such cases medical intervention may be advisable. Other times, however, your feelings of loneliness may result from your own hesitation to "get out there and make new friends."

Why might you hesitate to meet new people and make new friends? Perhaps you're naturally shy, and because of your shyness, you find it more difficult to interact with unfamiliar people. Or perhaps you're overly sensitive to the possibility of rejection. Oftentimes, this sensitivity to rejection results from low levels of self-esteem—you feel (quite incorrectly) that you are unworthy of the attentions of others.

In truth, the world is literally teeming with people who are looking for new friends like you. Unfortunately, many of those people are insecure and lonely, so if you want to meet them, it's up to you to make the effort.

Writer Suzanne Dale Ezell observed, "Friends are like a quilt with lots of different shapes, sizes, colors, and patterns of fabric.

But the end result brings you warmth and comfort in a support system that makes you life richer and fuller." And the American philosopher Ralph Waldo Emerson advised, "The only way to have a friend is to be one." Emerson realized that a lasting relationship, like a beautiful garden, must be tended with care. Here are a few helpful tips tending the garden of friendship . . . and reaping a bountiful harvest:

Lasting friendships are governed by a rule . . . the Golden Rule. The best way to keep a friend is to treat that person like you want to be treated. (Matthew 7:12)

If you're trying to make new friends, become interested in them . . . and eventually they'll become interested in you. (Colossians 3:12)

Friendships take time. It takes time to make new friendships and time to cultivate old one. But if you invest the time, you'll be glad you did . . . and so will they. (Philippians 1:3)

Get Involved: The more you involve yourself with various organizations (starting with your church), the better your chances to connect with lots of people. (1 Peter 5:2)

When I sit in darkness, the Lord will be a light to me.

MICAH 7:8 NKJV

You will be sad, but your sadness will become joy.

JOHN 16:20 NCV

Weeping may endure for a night, but joy comes in the morning.

PSALM 30:5 NKJV

*Behold, how good and how pleasant it is for brethren
to dwell together in unity!*

PSALM 133:1 NKJV

I am not alone, because the Father is with Me.

JOHN 16:32 NKJV

When we are living apart for God, we can be lonely and lost,
even in the midst of a crowd.

BILLY GRAHAM

Are you feeling lonely today because of suffering?
My word to you is simply this: Jesus Christ is there with you.

WARREN WIERSBE

Most loneliness results from insulation rather than isolation.

JAMES DOBSON

We are born helpless. As soon as we are fully conscious
we discover loneliness. We need others physically, emotionally,
intellectually; we need them if we are to know anything,
even ourselves.

C. S. LEWIS

ADDITIONAL BIBLE READINGS

HEBREWS 13:5; 2 CHRONICLES 16:9; JOSHUA 1:9; JAMES 4:8;

PSALM 139:7-10

LOSS OF PURPOSE

"Why did God put me here?" It's an easy question to ask and, at times, a very difficult question to answer. As you seek to answer that question, you should begin by remembering this: You are here because God put you here, and He has important work for you to do. But God's purposes will not always be clear to you. Sometimes you may wander aimlessly in a wilderness of your own making. And sometimes, you may struggle mightily against God in a vain effort to find success and happiness through your own means, not His.

Whenever we struggle against God's plans, we suffer. When we resist God's calling, our efforts bear little fruit. Our best strategy, therefore, is to seek God's wisdom and to follow Him wherever He chooses to lead. When we do so, we are blessed.

When we align ourselves with God's purposes, we avail ourselves of His power and His peace. But how can we know precisely what God's intentions are? The answer, of course, is that even the most well-intentioned believers face periods of uncertainty and doubt about the direction of their lives. So, too, will you.

When you arrive at one of life's inevitable crossroads, that is precisely the moment when you should turn your thoughts and prayers toward God. When you do, He will make Himself known to you in a time and manner of His choosing.

Are you earnestly seeking to discern God's purpose for your life? If so, remember these three points:

1. God has a plan for your life: If you believe that your life has no meaning, you are very wrong. God isn't finished with you yet, and He still has meaningful work for you to do. (Jeremiah 29:11)

2. If you seek God's plan sincerely and prayerfully, you will find it: God's plan for you may not be obvious, but neither is it incomprehensible. With prayer and patience, you can determine, with a surprising degree of clarity, the path that God intends for you to take. (Psalm 16:11)

3. When you discover God's purpose for your life, you will experience abundance, peace, joy, and power—God's power. And that's the only kind of power that really matters. (John 10:10; Psalm 84:5)

To everything there is a season,
a time for every purpose under heaven.

ECCLESIASTES 3:1 NKJV

God chose you to be his people, so I urge you now to live
the life to which God called you.

EPHESIANS 4:1 NCV

There is one thing I always do. Forgetting the past and straining
toward what is ahead, I keep trying to reach the goal and
get the prize for which God called me . . . .

PHILIPPIANS 3:13–14 NCV

You will show me the path of life; in Your presence is fullness of joy;
at Your right hand are pleasures forevermore.

PSALM 16:11 NKJV

More Thoughts About . . . **PURPOSE**

When God's glory is our reason for being, we are freed
from the entanglements of self-interest, self-promoting,
and self-centeredness. We are freed from the domination of sin
and liberated for our primary purpose.

SUSAN HUNT

To do good things in the world, first you must know
who you are and what gives meaning to your life.

PAULA BROWNLEE

We are all pencils in the hand of God.

MOTHER TERESA

God is more concerned with the direction of your life
than with its speed.

MARIE T. FREEMAN

ADDITIONAL BIBLE READINGS

PSALM 20:4; ROMANS 8:28; ROMANS 12:6-8; EPHESIANS 4:1;

GALATIANS 6:9; ROMANS 8:28

MATERIALISM

I n our modern society, we need money to live. But as Christians, we must never make the acquisition of money the central focus of our lives. Money is a tool, but it should never overwhelm our sensibilities. The focus of life must be squarely on things spiritual, not things material.

Whenever we place our love for material possessions above our love for God—or when we yield to the countless other temptations of everyday living—we find ourselves engaged in a struggle between good and evil. Let us respond to this struggle by freeing ourselves from that subtle yet powerful temptation: the temptation to love the world more than we love God.

Whenever we become absorbed with the acquisition of things, complications arise. Each new acquisition costs money or time, often both. To further complicate matters, many items can be purchased, not with real money, but with the something much more insidious: debt. Debt—especially consumer debt used to purchase depreciating assets—is a modern-day form of indentured servitude.

If you're looking for a sure-fire, time-tested way to simplify your life and thereby improve your world, learn to control your possessions before they control you. Purchase only those things that make a significant contribution to your well-being and the well-being of your family. Never spend more than you make.

Understand the folly in buying consumer goods on credit. Never use credit cards as a way of financing your lifestyle.

Ask yourself this simple question: "Do I own my possessions, or do they own me?" If you don't like the answer you receive, make an iron-clad promise to stop acquiring and start divesting. As you simplify your life, you'll be amazed at the things you can do without. You be pleasantly surprised at the sense of satisfaction that accompanies your new-found moderation. And you'll understand first-hand that when it comes to material possessions, less truly is more.

How important are our material possessions? Not as important as we might think. In the lives of committed Christians, material possessions should play a rather small role. Of course, we all need the basic necessities of life, but once we meet those needs for ourselves and for our families, the piling up of possessions creates more problems than it solves. Our real riches, of course, are not of this world. We are never really rich until we are rich in spirit.

Barbara Johnson observed, "The more we stuff ourselves with material pleasures, the less we seem to appreciate life." How true.

So, if you find yourself wrapped up in the concerns of the material world, it's time to reorder your priorities by turning your thoughts and your prayers to more important matters. And, it's time to begin storing up riches that will endure throughout eternity: the spiritual kind.

For what will it profit a man if he gains the whole world,
and loses his own soul?
Or what will a man give in exchange for his soul?

MARK 8:36-37 NKJV

He who trusts in his riches will fall,
but the righteous will flourish . . . .

PROVERBS 11:28 NKJV

Do not love the world or the things in the world.
If anyone loves the world, the love of the Father is not in him.

1 JOHN 2:15 NKJV

No one can serve two masters. The person will hate one master and
love the other, or will follow one master and refuse to follow the other.
You cannot serve both God and worldly riches.

MATTHEW 6:24 NCV

It's sobering to contemplate how much time, effort,
sacrifice, compromise, and attention we give to acquiring and
increasing our supply of something that is
totally insignificant in eternity.

ANNE GRAHAM LOTZ

As faithful stewards of what we have,
ought we not to give earnest thought to our staggering surplus?

ELISABETH ELLIOT

We are made spiritually lethargic by a steady diet
of materialism.

MARY MORRISON SUGGS

Money separates people more often than it joins them.

LIZ CURTIS HIGGS

ADDITIONAL BIBLE READINGS

MATTHEW 6:27-30; 1 TIMOTHY 6:6-10; HEBREWS 13:5; LUKE 12:15;

LUKE 12:19-21; LUKE 12:34; MARK 8:36-37

REJECTION

I f you're like most women, then you're sensitive to rejection. And if that description fits you, then you should be aware that the fear of rejection can be a major roadblock on the path to a purposeful life. Why? Because the more fearful you are of displeasing others, the more likely you are to make decisions that are not in your best interest.

When you try to please everybody in sight, you create for yourself a task that is unrealistic, unsatisfying, and unworthy of your efforts. A far better strategy, of course, is to concentrate, first and foremost, on pleasing God. But sometimes, that's easier said than done, especially if you focus too intently on being a "people pleaser."

Pleasing other people is a good thing . . . up to a point. Being a kind and considerate person is, of course, an important part of being a good Christian. But, you must never allow your "willingness to please" to interfere with our own good judgement or with God's commandments.

If you're a world-class people-pleaser—and if you're displeased with the consequences of your behavior—consider these points:

1. Your fear of rejection probably results from unspoken (yet highly pervasive) messages that you're telling yourself about the consequences of being judged "unworthy" or "imperfect" by the people whom you seek to impress. If so, it's time to start

thinking more about impressing God and less about impressing you pals. (2 Corinthians 5:9-10)

2. You may be living and laboring under the mistaken fear of saying the word "no" to other human beings. If so, your reluctance to say "no" may be standing between you and the things you want from life. So, summon the courage to use "no" every time that it's appropriate to do so. You'll be glad you did . . . and so, for that matter, will God.

You can't please everybody, nor should you even try. Of course there are a few people whom you should seek to please, starting with your family (and, to a lesser extent, the person who signs your paycheck). But, trying to please everybody else is an impossible, all-consuming task that will complicate your life, deplete your energies, and leave you unhappy, unappreciated, and unfulfilled.

So, focus your thoughts and energies on pleasing your Creator first and always. And when it comes to the world and all its inhabitants, don't worry too much about the folks you can't please. Focus, instead, on doing the right thing—and leave the rest up to God (Galatians 1:10).

Do you think I am trying to make people accept me?
No, God is the One I am trying to please.
Am I trying to please people? If I still wanted to please people,
I would not be a servant of Christ.

GALATIANS 1:10 NCV

But with me it is a very small thing that I should be judged by you or
by a human court. In fact, I do not even judge myself.
For I know nothing against myself, yet I am not justified by this;
but He who judges me is the Lord.

1 CORINTHIANS 4:3-4 NKJV

Our only goal is to please God whether we live here or there,
because we must all stand before Christ to be judged.

2 CORINTHIANS 5:9 NCV

You shall have no other gods before Me.

EXODUS 20:3 NKJV

More Thoughts About . . . PLEASING OTHERS AND PLEASING GOD

When you taste a measure of being able to love and enjoy
the people in your life, without having to have any particular
response from them, you are tasting bliss.

PAULA RINEHART

When we are set free from the bondage of pleasing others, when
we are free from currying others' favor and others' approval—
then no one will be able to make us miserable or dissatisfied.
And then, if we know we have pleased God,
contentment will be our consolation.

KAY ARTHUR

It is comfortable to know that we are responsible to God and
not to man. It is a small matter to be judged
of man's judgement.

LOTTIE MOON

People who constantly, and fervently, seek the approval of others
live with an identity crisis. They don't know who they are,
and they are defined by what others think of them.

CHARLES STANLEY

ADDITIONAL BIBLE READINGS

MARK 6:11; 1 CORINTHIANS 4:3-4; 2 CORINTHIANS 5:18; 2 TIMOTHY 2:4;

PROVERBS 11:25; TITUS 3:9

AFTER THE CRISIS

"For I will restore health to you and heal you of your wounds,"
says the Lord.

JEREMIAH 30:17 NKJV

Perhaps you're a woman who has picked up this book during a difficult time in your life. If so, don't lose hope. Sometime soon, perhaps sooner than you expect, the clouds will part, the sun will shine, and your crisis will pass. But the passing of your personal crisis *does not* mean that your spiritual journey has reached its completion. The path to spiritual maturity unfolds day by day. Each day offers the opportunity to worship God . . . or not. When you worship Him with your prayers, your words, your thoughts, and your actions, you will be blessed by the richness of your relationship with the Father.

Each day offers fresh opportunities for spiritual growth. If you choose, you can seize those opportunities by obeying God's Word, by seeking His will, and by walking with His Son. And as you begin your life "after the crisis," here are a few things to remember:

1. Learn the lessons; make the changes: Every crisis has lessons to teach. Your job is to learn those lessons *and* to make the necessary changes that *prove* you've learned those lessons. (Proverbs 9:9)

2. Remember that the healing continues after the crisis has passed: After a major life crisis, don't expect instantaneous healing—expect a few emotional aftershocks. From time to time, you may find yourself dwelling *on* the past—but don't dwell *in* the past. And if your emotional aftershocks become too intense, seek help. (Psalm 27:14)

3. Get connected; get involved: After the crisis, it will be your responsibility to engage yourself with people and organizations that provide the enrichment and support you need. Whether it's your local church, a neighborhood service organization, or a local support group, get involved: you need *their* help . . . and *they* need yours. (1 Thessalonians 5:11)

4. If the problem recurs, you'll be better prepared when it does: sometimes, Old Man Trouble has a way of rearing his head over and over again. But if Mister Trouble *does* return to your house, you can take comfort in the fact that after this crisis, you are now better prepared to meet him, to greet him, and to usher him out the door . . . quickly! (Hebrews 12:11)

5. Share what you've learned: Other people will endure the same hardships you've faced, and they need the benefit of your experiences *now*. Remember: the best way to keep your wisdom fresh is to give it away every day. (Titus 2:7)

6. God has a plan and a path; keep searching for that plan, and keep following His path: God has a unique purpose for your life, and He has a path that He intends for you to take in order to fulfill that purpose. Seek the purpose; walk the path. (Psalm 32:8)

If you're one of those women who sincerely want to discover God's path, it's up to you to learn the lessons that tough times can teach. And it's up to you to make changes—*and* choices—that are pleasing to your Creator. He deserves no less . . . and neither, for that matter, do you.

NOTES

ABOUT CRISWELL FREEMAN

Criswell Freeman's books have sold millions of copies, yet his name is largely unknown to the general public. *The Wall Street Journal* observed, "Normally, a tally like that would put a writer on the best-seller lists. But Freeman is hardly a household name." And that's exactly how the author likes it.

The Washington Post called Freeman "possibly the most prolific 'quote book' writer in America." With little fanfare, Dr. Freeman has compiled and edited well over a hundred titles that have now sold over 8,000,000 copies.

Freeman began his writing career as a self-help author (his first book was entitled *When Life Throws You a Curveball, Hit It*). Today, Freeman's writings focus on the Good News of God's Holy Word. Criswell is a Doctor of Clinical Psychology (he earned his degree from the Adler School of Professional Psychology in Chicago). He earned his undergraduate degree at Vanderbilt University. Freeman also attended classes at The Southern Baptist Theological Seminary in Louisville where he studied under the noted pastoral counselor Wayne Oates.

Criswell lives in Nashville, Tennessee. He is married and has two daughters.

ABOUT CONNIE WETZELL

Connie Wetzell is an award winning radio personality, voice-over artist, author and speaker. She is the Author and Voice-over artist on "The Healing Word of God" CD series and the voice-over artist and producer of the audio version of "The Women of Faith Devotional Bible" by Thomas Nelson Bibles.